THE GREAT DEPRESSION
AND THE NEW DEAL

ANNE E. SCHRAFF

THE GREAT DEPRESSION AND THE NEW DEAL

AMERICA'S ECONOMIC COLLAPSE AND RECOVERY

FOREWORD BY
ELLIOTT ROOSEVELT

Barbara Silberdick Feinberg,
Consulting Editor

FRANKLIN WATTS
A TWENTIETH CENTURY
AMERICAN HISTORY BOOK
NEW YORK LONDON TORONTO
SYDNEY 1990

973. 917
Schraff

Library of Congress Cataloging-in-Publication Data

Schraff, Anne E.
The Great Depression and the New Deal : America's economic
collapse and recovery / Anne E. Schraff.
p.   cm. — (A Twentieth century American history book)
Includes bibliographical references (p.   ).
Summary: Discusses the devastating effect of the 1929 stock market
crash on American economy and Franklin D. Roosevelt's programs to
restore the nation's financial health.
ISBN 0-531-10964-X
1. New Deal, 1933–1939—Juvenile literature.
2. Depressions—1929—United States—Juvenile literature.   3. United
States—History—1933–1945—Juvenile literature.
4. United States—Economic policy—1939–1945—Juvenile literature.
5. United States—History—1919–1933—
Juvenile literature. [1. Depressions—1929.
2. New Deal, 1933–1939. 3. United States—Economic
policy—1933–1945.] I. Title. II. Series.
E806.S356   1990
973.917—dc20   90-34699   CIP   AC

For Dr. Francis W. Schruben,
an inspiring history teacher

CONTENTS

Foreword by Elliott Roosevelt
9

Chapter One
Storm Clouds Gather
11

Chapter Two
The Bubble Bursts
17

Chapter Three
The Depression Deepens
28

Chapter Four
The Rise and Fall of the Bonus Army
35

Chapter Five
The March to Victory
41

Chapter Six
The First "Hundred Days"—Part One
52

Chapter Seven
The First "Hundred Days"—Part Two
58

Chapter Eight
Minorities in the Depression
68

Chapter Nine
Drums of Discontent—The Second New Deal
73

Chapter Ten
A Last Act and Assessment
84

———

Highlights of the Great Depression
and the New Deal
97

Photography Credits
99

Notes
100

Bibliography
104

Index
108

FOREWORD

Anne E. Schraff has created, in this short and readable account of the greatest depression in United States history, a book that should become required reading in every high school throughout our country.

I, frankly, was surprised and pleased with this material when I sat down to read it. It is not a slanted account, as so often happens when historical writers let their pens take over to get their viewpoint across.

I lived through that entire era. I saw with my own eyes the tarpaper shacks where the homeless lived on the West Side of New York City, and the endless lines of hopeless humans lined up at the soup kitchens. I listened to the frustrated farmers venting their wrath when their milk, eggs, meat, and vegetables were bringing in pennies instead of dollars. As the president's son, I traveled all the way across the country to get a job, because there weren't any where I lived.

There is no exaggeration in Schraff's telling of the events leading up to our economic collapse. The fact that the whole business structure collapsed and crushed the hopes and lifetime aspirations of all but the super-rich is factually presented. The fact that President Roosevelt's New Deal cohorts were adept at coming up with new and ever more far-reaching panaceas that would restart the economic machine and bring us back to prosperity is accurately related. The fact that between 1933 and 1940 none of the panaceas actually did what was intended for them, but that the spirit and hopes of the people revived and became enthused with their own future potentials, is detailed honestly and fairly.

President Roosevelt orchestrated the New Deal program. He was determined to preserve the pride of the American workers in their own ability to earn their living. So he steered clear of welfare and giving money to the unemployed, and he concentrated on creating jobs for the people. His "alphabet soup" agencies—PWA, WPA, CCC, TVA, and NYA—all worked toward providing permanent improvements on the America of the future. The resulting improvements were terribly slow, but the faith of our citizenry revived, and this was the most important victory.

One conclusion from this recitation of a portion of our history is quite evident. The generations of tomorrow must never permit our free-enterprise capitalist system to ever come to a grinding halt again, as it did in 1929. It would take a major war, as it did then, to bring us back to full prosperity and save our system.

Please God that those of today's and tomorrow's generations will learn this simple lesson well. You must all be aware and prepared so that no repetition of those terrible years can ever confront us again.

Elliott Roosevelt

1

STORM CLOUDS GATHER

On May 20, 1927, a shy, handsome young pilot left Roosevelt Field on Long Island, New York, on a plane named the *Spirit of St. Louis*. Charles A. Lindbergh would fly the first solo, nonstop, transatlantic flight in history, landing thirty-three and a half hours later in France.

"Am I in Paris?" were the twenty-five-year-old American's first words after he landed.

"You're here!" answered the astonished French crowds. It was another unbelievable event in what was one of America's most dramatic decades—the Roaring Twenties. When Lindbergh returned to New York, eighteen hundred tons of ticker tape rained down on him. A new hero had been crowned, and flight had become part of the cultural scene.

During the 1920s, Americans enjoyed a love affair with the automobile. By 1923, 23 million Ford Model T Tin Lizzies had been sold. By 1927, 15 million Lizzies cruised down American highways. Used Model T's could be purchased for ten dollars. The city worker could now live farther from his place of employment and drive to work, and the family could go on weekend jaunts. Filling stations, service garages, gift shops, and tourist camps sprang up like weeds on newly built highways and byways to accommodate a brisker pace of life. Farmers attached a pickup truck device and hauled their crops to market in the Model T. By jacking up the rear wheel and using a homemade attachment, the farmer could even use the engine to saw wood.

All kinds of amazing gadgets were quickly becoming part of the American way of life. Electric vacuum cleaners and washing machines and radios became common. Pittsburgh's KDKA was the first commercial broadcast station on the air in December 1920. Within four years as many as 562 stations offered a wide selection of music, stock market and news reports, bedtime stories, church services, and prizefights. A newspaper editor commented that every night was filled with radio music.

The silent movies had already dazzled people with stars like Charlie Chaplin and Mary Pickford. In October 1927, Al Jolson sang and spoke in *The Jazz Singer*. The age of the talkies had begun. Jack Dempsey was heavyweight boxing champion, and Babe Ruth was hitting home runs for the New York Yankees.

It was the era of Prohibition—a bright, gaudy time, with gangsters riding high from riches gained through selling bootleg liquor (since it was illegal to sell liquor in public saloons, illegal or bootleg liquor was sold in behind-the-scenes establishments called speakeasies). A defiant, rebellious spirit ran through American youth. Girls bobbed (cut short) their hair, rouged their cheeks, and rolled down their stockings, favoring lean, boyish styles and short skirts. It had required nineteen yards of fabric to make a dress in 1919; in the twenties seven yards sufficed. The feverish spirit of Jazz Age youth was effectively captured by F. Scott Fitzgerald, the twenty-four-year-old author of *This Side of Paradise* and other novels of the decade.

America seemed to be having the party of her life and hardly anybody was thinking that it might end soon. *Time* magazine of January 1929 featured Walter P. Chrysler as the man of the year. He'd just introduced the new Plymouth and DeSoto cars, and he was building a brand-new skyscraper. The wealthy of the twenties lived in true grandeur in $45,000 apartments with bathrooms equipped with gold-plated fixtures. Rich men spurned two-dollar Arrow shirts for twenty-dollar silk shirts.

But the well-to-do were not alone in acting as if the party would go on forever. Just about everybody believed anything was possible in such times. You could buy what your heart desired if you had the cash or not. Cars, furniture, clothing, and jewelry could be purchased on the installment plan—a small down payment and the balance owed in easy monthly payments. The common saying of the times was "A dollar down and a dollar when they catch you." You could enjoy it now and pay for it later.

Many embarked on the royal road to riches by playing the stock market. Anybody could play by buying on margin. This meant you could place a small amount of cash, about 10 percent of what the stock share cost, with a broker, who would make up the difference. Shoe-shine boys were buying $100 worth of stock for $8 and $10. Stocks were rising in value so fast that "becoming rich as Rockefeller" seemed within the grasp of ordinary people. Teenaged typists and stenographers, small shopkeepers, and the retired joined the mad buying spree.

In the White House sat President Herbert Hoover, a self-made man who was living proof of the American dream. A rugged individualist, Hoover believed that the common interest of society is served by allowing individuals freedom to work hard on their own, without government interference. Hoover was a poor orphan boy who had become rich and famous in just this way, through hard work and ingenuity. In 1929 he told the American people, "We in America today are nearer the final triumph over poverty than ever before in any land."

Still, even at the height of the roaring optimism of the 1920s, ominous clouds had begun to gather. Farm prices had collapsed in 1924. South Dakota corn sold for less than 3¢ a bushel in 1928–29. The farmers couldn't afford to sell at this price, so they used it as fuel to keep warm. Other farmers killed hogs they could not sell for a break-even price. In some areas farmers were so desperate they were tearing the seat covers from their cars to make clothing for their children.

Other industries were in trouble, too. In 1926 hard times hit the coal mines and lumber mills. The growing use of fuel oil and natural gas forced coal prices down. Coal companies turned to cheaper nonunion mines in the South, putting northern miners out of work. Lumbermen protested low wages, causing unrest in the lumber industry.

Throughout America there was a dangerous imbalance of wealth. In 1929, 42.4 percent of Americans worked hard at their jobs while earning less than $1,500 a year. That wasn't enough to keep up with inflation (rapid increases of prices above the real value of the product). Wage earners could buy less and less with each dollar they earned. While the production of the American worker increased during the 1920s, their wages did not keep pace. Too much income went toward profits for the wealthy. The auto worker made more cars during his workweek, but he was becoming less able to buy one for his own family. That year 26 percent of the nation's wealth went to just 5 percent of its people.

Just as the stock market was a dream machine for many Americans, it was also a roller coaster. It rose to the dizzying heights of an amusement park's most frightening ride, but the plunge was just as inevitable. Yet nobody wanted to believe that. Gullible people entered the gamble in ever-greater numbers in the late twenties. Brokers opened branches of their offices near college campuses and in small towns. Widows eking out a living on a small pension or living on interest from a modest bank account were lured into investing most, if not all, of their security in the stock market.

Brand-new, shaky companies were formed, and stocks in these companies were sold cheap, with promises of rich rewards when the companies flourished. The innocents who bought such stock knew nothing about the risks of business failures. Crooked traders on Wall Street started false rumors to raise or lower prices so that insiders could make huge killings. Fortunes were made on whispers in the halls. One economist called it "honeyfugling, hornswoggling and skulduggery," but the naive men and women on Main Street dreamed on.

The world economy was another dark cloud on the horizon of America's prosperity. At the conclusion of World War I in 1919, the Treaty of Versailles was signed to dictate the terms of peace. Germany had lost the war, and now she had to admit it was entirely her fault and pay the price. Germany lost many of her economic resources and was ordered to pay billions of dollars in war reparations to the Allies, primarily France and Great Britain. The German economy floundered. Eventually, since the nations of Europe are intertwined economically by trade, the economic disaster in Germany spread to other nations in Europe. Long before the bubble of American prosperity burst, Germany was struggling with hard times.

Adding to the world's economic woes were the stiff tariff policies of Presidents Harding and Coolidge, who preceded Hoover. (Tariffs are taxes on goods imported from other countries.) American businessmen did not want competition from foreign-made goods, and American workers feared that foreign-made goods posed a danger to their jobs, too. In 1922, U.S. tariffs were increased and kept high. Since foreign goods were less welcome in America, Europe retaliated by keeping American goods out of their markets. The high tariff policies of the 1920s played havoc with the whole system of international trade.

Although President Hoover said Americans ought to "anticipate the future with optimism" and although the arrival of 1929 was toasted with illegal champagne to the strains of the latest dance band, the handwriting was already on the wall. The roller coaster had reached the breathtaking summit of its ride, and a still-screaming, joyous America now stared into the horrifying abyss that would shake the nation to its foundations. Those who lived through the next decade would never be quite the same again. America would be changed forever.

2

THE BUBBLE BURSTS

Promptly at 10:00 A.M. Thursday, October 24, 1929, the gong of the New York Stock Exchange sounded. Six thousand shares of Montgomery Ward sold for $83 a share. The shares were down from $156. Stocks were plunging two to ten points between transactions. Panic was spreading, and soon the floor of the New York Stock Exchange was filled with milling, screaming men, their faces alabaster white with fear. The day would be known as "Black Thursday," the day the bubble of American prosperity burst.

Why now? Why on this particular Thursday? Had the economy bloated to such an extent that, like a hot-air balloon, it was just waiting to burst? Or had one gloomy prediction triggered the bust? On September 5, 1929, Roger W. Babson said, "There is a crash coming, and it may be a terrific one." Babson, a financial statistician, was denounced by economists as an alarmist, but others joined Babson in warning that too much stock in too many questionable companies had been sold and too many unwise bank loans had been made. When the Crash came, some grumbled that Babson and the other doomsayers were to blame. They'd scared the stock market to death!

At 1:30 P.M., Richard Whitney, a broker and sports-man, strode through the maddened crowd. U.S. Steel was plunging like a tin can over Niagara Falls. It was down to $190 a share when Whitney stunned everyone by offering $205 a share for 25,000 shares. The incredible plunge had been halted, and some vainly believed that a disaster had been averted. The humorist Will Rogers wrote in his column that the wealthy fellows had pulled some strings and now the market was perking right up. But not even J.P. Morgan and all the other tycoons plotting strategies at high-level huddles could stop this runaway freight train now. The mad rush to sell stocks had taken on a life of its own, and blind fear ruled the day. An investor who had seen his stock go down from $100 to $50 in one day could not be convinced to hold it until tomor-row on the chance it might rise. He was simply too fright-ened that it would be $25 or less tomorrow. The frantic selling of stock was like a rush of people fleeing a burning building. People were too afraid to make orderly lines, so they trampled the stock market in their desperation to salvage what they could. [1]

The worst was yet to come. Weeping brokers tore off their collars to enable quicker tallying. Their blood pres-sure had gone so high that the collars seemed to be chok-ing them. One trader stayed in his office with his tapes running nonstop for days. Stocks were going on the mar-ket so fast that their prices sank more quickly than the stock market ticker could record them. At one time the tickers were a full two hours behind the current prices. In a matter of two days, hundreds of thousands of Americans had been transformed from comfortable investors to beg-gars and debtors.

Newsboys ran up and down the streets of every major American city screaming, "Stock market crashes." Hun-dreds of wealthy American tourists were in Paris at the time, and now they were stranded without the money to return home. Their fortunes lost in the Crash, they lacked even steamship fare for the return voyage. Days before, they had been buying expensive furs and gems. Now they sold these same items for half what they paid just in order to get home.[2]

John D. Rockefeller, Jr., tried to stem the panic by assuring everyone that he and his sons continued to buy stocks as usual. It was to no avail. A General Motors stock that sold for $91 before the Crash went for $30 the day after. By 1932 this stock would be selling for $7. U.S. Steel stock dropped from a high of $261 to $150 after the crash. They then dropped to $21 in 1932. Within weeks, one-and-a-half million Americans had lost $30 billion on the stock market. This was about one-third of the gross national product of the country. It was the most devastating financial collapse in American history.

One steel executive's story was typical of his generation. He lost most of his money in the Crash, though he had enough left to live frugally. Once, he had been vitally interested in art, politics, and the world around him. Now he spent his days staring blankly into space as if he'd seen a ghost and would never be able to forget the horror of it. One wealthy company president sat ashen faced at his desk and said, "I don't have two dimes left to rub together."

Americans who had been well-off and found themselves suddenly impoverished suffered anxiety attacks. Psychiatrists were overwhelmed with work, but some people could not be helped and ended their lives in rest homes or mental hospitals.[3]

By the end of 1929, the entire American economy had followed the stock market into ruin. Consumer buying declined sharply. People had their hours cut, and then their wages. They dared not buy new clothing. It was wiser to patch what they already had. Extra amenities in the family budget were canceled. People stopped buying radios and suits, washing machines, and cars. Then the vicious cycle moved with quickening speed. Because there was less demand, car and radio manufacturers were forced to cut back hours and wages. The dreaded pink slip told hundreds, then thousands, that their jobs were gone.

People moved to cheaper quarters or moved in with relatives. Aged couples found their long-married children coming home to set up housekeeping in the attic, the basement, the spare room. One Italian family had ten children, with their spouses and *their* children all back under the family roof. The quality of food dropped until meat was a once-a-week luxury. Whereas steaks were once common at daily meals, now there was bologna.

The America of 1929 had no unemployment insurance, no Social Security, no programs now called the social safety nets that are supposed to cushion the blows of hard times. Either your relatives or friends helped, or you turned to local charities. And such a large disaster quickly strained the resources of all local and private charities. It is hard to imagine it today, but for the out-of-work American of the depression there was absolutely no government program to fall back on in 1929.

As men lost their jobs and couldn't find another, many of them took to the road in a desperate search for work. They assured themselves that conditions down the road couldn't be as bad as they were at home. But they soon found that the depression had beaten them to the next town, too. Many slept in hobo jungles and cheap hotels called flophouses. They slept in parks and along the roadside and ate in bread lines and soup lines, or else they scavenged food from the backs of restaurants or city dumps. Makeshift camps, made of flattened tin cans and torn-up sheets of iron, swiftly rose up. They were dubbed

Hoovervilles in honor of the president many had begun to blame for this misfortune.

Influential Americans from President Hoover on down continued to believe the depression could be resolved by a big dose of cheerfulness. There is some truth to this because lack of confidence was making a bad situation worse. Even people who could afford to buy radios or a new pair of shoes refused to do so because they feared they might need those extra dollars if things got worse. Optimism on the part of many Americans would have eased the situation if only it could have been roused. The dapper mayor of New York, Jimmy Walker, did his part by asking the nation's theaters to show only happy movies. The National Association of Manufacturers put up billboards featuring pretty girls proclaiming: "Business is good. Keep it good. Nothing can stop U.S." And President Hoover became head cheerleader. In November 1929 he said, "Business and industry have turned the corner." In January 1930 he said, "We have now passed the worst." But the president's cheerfulness was met by gallows humor from embittered Americans who felt they were on a sinking ship with sharks circling and a buffoon at the helm who insisted that all was well despite water bubbling at his kneecaps.

President Hoover firmly believed that things would get better with little or no help from the government. Many people felt this way since depressions in the past seemed to resolve themselves in time. But there had never been one so enormous as this. Sadly, this much-hated president, now being blamed for the rising tide of human misery engulfing the nation, was a great humanitarian who anguished over the tragedy of suffering people. He had headed up the highly successful relief program for starving Europeans during World War I. He had helped displaced Mississippians cope with a terrible flood back in 1927.

Hoover, the orphan son of an Iowa blacksmith, had worked a seven-day week in a gold mine as a youth. Unemployed and poor himself, he learned "the bottom levels of real human despair." But through hard struggle he managed to pull himself up by his own bootstraps and pay his way through Stanford University. He eventually became a successful mining engineer and gained wealth and fame. Like many such men whose lives were inspiring success stories of "poor boys making good," he believed anybody else could do as well if they just exerted the effort. Hoover was convinced that with good old American know-how and volunteerism, the depression could be beaten, just as young Herbert Hoover overcame his own personal setbacks.

When others suggested that the federal government had to take drastic action against the monster depression, Hoover threw up his hands in horror. What? Bring on socialism? Under socialism there is government ownership of the land and means of production and distribution. Fewer decisions are in the hands of individuals. Hoover saw this as the road to tyranny. No, he thought, Americans could handle this themselves with just a bit of help from local and private charities. Hoover suggested volunteers to launch "give a job" campaigns. He urged cities to start public works projects to employ the jobless. "If you let the federal government help the individual," Hoover warned, "soon the federal government will control that individual." Andrew Mellon, Hoover's secretary of the treasury, went so far as to say it wasn't a bad thing if everything went right to the bottom. "People will work harder," he said, "live a more moral life. Values will be adjusted and enterprising people will pick up the wrecks from less competent people."

The flaw in logic of this kind was that the depression was too large for solutions that had worked before in lesser economic hard times. Private and local agencies were swamped. They were not organized for a disaster of this magnitude. Since so many people were unemployed, state and local taxes plummeted, leaving city and state governments even less able to provide help. With so many Americans suddenly impoverished, charities received fewer gifts. Organizations like the Salvation Army were used to caring for those few down-and-out people always living on the edge of society. Now just about everyone needed help. Asking local government and private charities to solve the problems of the depression was like asking mice to stop a herd of stampeding elephants. New York City could afford only $2.39 a week for a family of four. Smaller, poorer cities could afford nothing at all.

Still, President Hoover insisted, "We suffer from frozen confidence, not frozen securities." He could not overcome a lifetime of belief that the individual could do anything if he tried hard enough. But the American people had lost confidence in themselves, in the nation, and most assuredly in President Hoover.

One of the most grueling signs of the depression in the last days of 1929 was the soup line. Cities were doing the best they could with dwindling resources. The soup was often so thin that it was called "make believe" soup. Everybody brought their own buckets, and the first in line got mostly water. The ones farther down the line were luckier. They might even get some taste to their soup. Sunk deep in the huge pots were meat and potatoes, and the lucky few at the end might get a potato or a hunk of meat. Bread lines offered stale bread, and some tried to kill the taste with mustard.

To the growing army of unemployed men—fathers and husbands with families to support—the soup kitchen was a big pot along the Santa Fe Railroad line. Into it would go anything anybody had, from cabbage to beans. Everybody dipped out a portion. White and black stood together in a brotherhood of misery that would have astonished them in more prosperous times.

How could a country as wealthy as the United States have come to this? People had grown up believing that if you worked hard, kept your nose to the grindstone, and did your duty, things would work out. Only loafers and those of low moral character found themselves jobless and homeless. But somehow all the rules had been changed. Right in the middle of the game of life they had all understood so well, without warning or reason, the rules had been changed. And not just in America. The depression had struck Austria, Brazil, Asia, Argentina, Canada, and Poland, among others. In Germany conditions were turning grim, and the economic misery was spreading to Great Britain, France, Czechoslovakia, Switzerland, and Scandinavia. But it was in Germany that the evils of depression were hatching an even more monstrous wrong.

No nation was more vulnerable to a depression than Germany. The sharp cut in world trade hurt Germany badly. In September 1929, nearly a million and a half Germans were unemployed. In one year that number had doubled. Cold and hunger settled in, with young people leaving school with no hope of a job and all citizens losing their sense of self-worth. As the hopes and dreams of a nation crumbled, a man with piercing, demonic eyes and a harsh, passionate voice—Adolf Hitler—rose to power. He offered hope to his desperate people. He told the German people that all their suffering was due to the speculators and wicked money men.[4] There were voices in America delivering similar messages. Desperate people listen to the ravings of demagogues (unprincipled people who play on the ignorance and prejudice of people). Germany was ripe for Hitler, and if something wasn't done soon in America, some feared that the democratic system in the United States would be in serious jeopardy, too.

President Hoover tried to encourage farm cooperatives and strengthen farm credit through the Agricultural Marketing Act of 1929. It created the Federal Farm Board with a fund of $500 million. This money would be loaned to groups of farmers so that they could market their products more efficiently, build warehouses, and hold farm products for higher prices. As wheat and cotton prices skidded wildly, the Grain Stabilization Board and the Cotton Stabilization Board bought up grain and cotton in the hopes of raising prices. The Federal Farm Board tried to persuade farmers to limit production, but they couldn't compel them to do so. Unfortunately, warehouses filled to overflowing with products nobody could buy. The plan failed, and the situation on the farms went from bad to worse. Rural leaders were talking about violent remedies for farmers faced with foreclosures and losses of farms that had been in the family for generations. Adding to the misery was the drought of 1930 in the lower Mississippi Valley, Arkansas, and areas along the Ohio and Potomac rivers.

In April 1930, 3 million Americans were unemployed. To create new jobs, President Hoover asked Congress for $700 million for public improvements that had been scheduled for later. After all, Hoover reasoned, these were needed public roads, harbors, and public buildings, so there was no harm in just moving them ahead a bit to ease unemployment. Hoover then met with business and labor leaders and asked them to make voluntary agreements to hold off wage reductions and layoffs. The factory owners tried to comply, but who could afford to keep workers making products nobody was buying?

Some businessmen argued that foreign goods allowed into the United States would only hurt the national economy. If the government would ban foreign imports, then American consumers would use American products exclusively. It was faulty reasoning, but it took hold of the imagination of Congress. Even though high tariffs in the past had hurt everybody as nations retaliated against one another, many still believed they could work. Those favoring extreme protectionism (protecting American businesses by keeping foreign products out) led a drumbeat of agitation for still higher tariffs. The Smoot-Hawley Tariff Bill of June 1930 was passed despite the pleas of a thousand economists. The American trade door, open barely a crack before, now just about slammed tight. Foreign nations did what everybody, even Hoover, knew they would. Great Britain ended her historic free-trade policy, and other nations followed. It was full-scale trade war as nations struck back at high American tariffs by raising their own tariffs. American exports were cut in half. And the unemployment picture for Americans grew even grimmer.

As 1930 limped dismally along, Americans often found they couldn't even pay their one-dollar-a-month electric bills. Kerosene lamps, once discarded in favor of progress, returned to homes. White-collar workers took more salary cuts in the hopes of at least saving their jobs. While vacations and trips to the theater and baseball games plummeted, Americans did manage to scrape up the money for movies. Here, for a little while, in dark movie houses, there was escape from the harsh realities of the depression. Moviegoers relived the horror of World War I in All Quiet on the Western Front and saw Edward G. Robinson in the first of a long line of gangster pictures, Little Caesar. Gaudy escapist fare like The Vagabond King and Harold Lloyd comedies were big favorites. But there were many Americans who couldn't even afford a brief trip to tinsel land. On New York's Bowery, thousands stood in bread lines.

As 1930 drew to a close, the International Apple Shippers Association came up with a novel scheme to dispose of surplus apples. They sold the apples on credit to jobless people. The apples retailed on the street for five cents per apple, giving a small profit to the shippers and a living for the sellers. By November 1930, 6,000 apple sellers stood on the streets of New York. The apple seller became a symbol of the desperation of the unemployed. The apple growers had a good idea—it was the kind of thing President Hoover hoped would happen all over: creative ideas on the part of business. But it was a small stopgap measure, not a broad solution. By Christmas of 1930 in America, there was little to celebrate. Not Hoover's few programs, not all the forced optimism, could obscure the growing tragedy.

3

THE DEPRESSION
DEEPENS

Six million unemployed Americans greeted the New Year in January 1931. The popular song making the rounds— "Life Is Just a Bowl of Cherries"—sounded hollow to those who didn't know where their next meal was coming from.

President Hoover enjoyed a brief break from the unrelieved gloom of his office in May 1931 as he attended the gala official opening of the Empire State Building in New York. The new skyscraper was hailed as the tallest building in existence and the eighth wonder of the world. At 102 stories, the very top was a mooring mast for dirigibles (self-propelled steerable balloons or blimps). The building had 6,400 windows and 7 miles of elevator shafts. The doom-sayers of the times said the Empire State Building would become a gruesome monument to dying capitalism, standing like the hollow skeleton of a prehistoric animal.

Also in New York, the luxurious Waldorf-Astoria Hotel was opening, and stubborn optimists insisted that one day both the skyscraper and the hotel would be packed with people again enjoying prosperous times. It was hard to believe that in the summer of 1931.

Newspapers described the "yellowing" of Broadway. It wasn't that it didn't come alive every night with people as usual, but it was a different sort of crowd. Instead of animated groups of theatergoers bedecked in furs and jewels, there were people getting handouts from relief trucks. The largest truck was owned by the newspaperman William Randolph Hearst, and lines stretched for blocks when free food was passed out.

In Chicago, men and women who could no longer afford their own doctors came to free clinics. Even more unlucky Chicagoans fainted from hunger on the streetcars.

The depression struck black Chicagoans with special cruelty. Many had come to the North to escape discriminatory jobs and to find better wages. Jobless families were now being evicted from their homes, and groups were formed to try to stop the evictions. On one dingy, ill-kempt street a woman had just been evicted, and her small pile of possessions stood on the sidewalk. The neighborhood committee put her things back in the house. Then a roar of anguish went up as another family down the street was being evicted. As the committee tried to restore them to their house, two squads of police cars arrived. The police sergeant drew his gun, and a young black man confronted him. "You can't shoot all of us," said the young man, "so you might as well shoot me. All we want is to see that these people get back in their homes. We have no money, no jobs, sometimes no food. We've got to live someplace." The sergeant holstered his gun and went away. [1]

In Wisconsin, angry hunger marchers filed past city hall. Only the local duck hunters sharing their bounty from the woods with their neighbors averted serious malnutrition for many families.

In cities all over America sheriffs were evicting people who hadn't paid their rent or mortgage payments. In other homes unpaid-for furniture was being carted away. A houseful of furniture could be lost if the recent installment hadn't been paid, even if only $30 remained on a bill of $200.

One repossessor (a person who takes goods back from a buyer who has failed to make payments when due) recalled going into homes where the family dinner rested on the table. He had to put the plates on the floor before taking the table. Some sympathetic collectors would leave the beds at least, telling their employers that the mattresses were too full of cockroaches to be worth reclaiming. Often the repossessor faced the wrath of desperate people. One man met the repossessor at the top of the stairs with a rifle. An elderly woman screamed bloody murder as her last and most loved possession was taken away—her radio. Some people chopped up sofas and divans with razor blades, knives, and saws before the repossessor got to them. [2]

In San Francisco, when the Spreckles Sugar Refinery offered four jobs, a thousand people showed up.

In June 1931, Germany's president, Paul von Hindenburg, appealed to President Hoover to declare a moratorium (a period of respite) on intergovernmental debts. Germany was facing immediate financial collapse. Hoover wisely agreed, and the moratorium was accepted by other nations as well. A small measure of stability was restored to Germany and the world economy, but it was only temporary. For Germany, doomsday would wait a little while more.

In the fall of 1931 President Hoover received the frightening news that great manufacturing and utility corporations, insurance companies, building and loan associations, banks, railroads, and charitable groups were on the verge of bankruptcy. Thirty-six hundred banks had already failed, costing thousands of investors their life savings. There were no effective banking safeguards at the time. Thrifty people put their small savings in the bank against a rainy day, and the banks loaned this money out, often foolishly. As a result, as people couldn't repay the loans, banks failed and money was lost. Seven railroads had already gone bankrupt, too. Unless something was done, the entire American economic structure threatened to collapse. How could America ever recover if most of her companies were out of business?

Greatly alarmed by the ominous new threat, President Hoover called on Congress to create the Reconstruction Finance Corporation to lend large sums of money to banks, railroads, and other businesses. Some called it "the breadline for business," but few really argued with Hoover's drastic measures to save these large companies. But when a congressman said, "If we are giving direct relief to corporations, why not direct relief to the poor?" A bill was passed to provide this relief but President Hoover vetoed it. He felt the federal government could extend help to large industries without endangering the American economy, but the thought of federal relief checks going directly to individuals continued to frighten him. Relief had to be a local matter, he said, arguing that he was defending American principles.

Desperation deepened with hard times. Communist agitators were appearing more frequently at hunger marches and union meetings. America seemed to some to be ripe for revolution. How much longer were people going to put up with such misery? Many believed in 1931 that both America and Germany would soon have Communist revolutions. In Germany, men, women, and children fought over the contents of garbage pails, and day by day Hitler's movement grew stronger.

Black sharecroppers (tenant farmers who till land for

the owner in return for a share of the produce) formed unions to defend themselves against the exploitation of landlords. Several died in violent confrontations with local sheriffs in Alabama. Other farmers also decided to take the law into their own hands. In a last-ditch effort to raise farm prices and give themselves enough profit to make a living, they banded together. If their government couldn't help them, they'd help themselves.

The farmers formed Holiday associations to stop selling anything until prices were forced up. The motto was Neither Buy Nor Sell, and Let the Taxes Go to Hell. Picket lines were formed across major highways. They stopped milk wagons and dumped the milk into ditches. They turned back fellow farmers who would sell their hogs for two cents a pound. The Holiday farmers were armed with pitchforks, and any wheeled vehicle coming through ended up with punctured tires.

Some farmers tried to get through with teams of horses. "I'm only trying to feed my family," a farmer would plead as he tried to exchange a few dozen eggs and a few pounds of cream for meat. He'd be turned back with everyone else. Thirteen highways to Sioux Falls, South Dakota, were blocked, and the stockyards were emptied in two days. If the farmers were going to lose their shirts, by golly, nobody else was going to eat pork chops and steaks. One time, deputies came along with a fleet of trucks taking produce to market. One lone farmer had laid planks across the road. The armed deputies ordered him to remove the planks or they would be forced to shoot him. The farmer said to go ahead and shoot, "but there isn't any one of you getting out of here alive." Fifteen hundred gun-toting farmers were hiding in the woods along the highway. When the deputies looked around to see the trees alive with farmers, they turned the convoy of trucks around, and nothing got to market.[3]

For Americans who still had jobs, even at lowered wages, there was the ever-present fear of who would be next to lose their job. Like some silent plague striking down its victims, the depression lurked in every family's nightmares. The diversions of the time, offering distractions from the gnawing fears of tomorrow, included magazines like *True Story*, pulp western and detective books, and the *Reader's Digest*. Gangster Al Capone stood in a sober blue suit to be sentenced for income tax evasion. Most Americans marveled that *anybody* was still making enough money to owe sizable taxes. Meanwhile, the Marx Brothers tried to create a few laughs in a movie called *Monkey Business*, and Charlie Chaplin was a believable and lovable tramp in *City Lights*.

As 1932 arrived, the new popular song was "Brother, Can You Spare a Dime?" It fit the mood of the nation perfectly. Between 1930 and 1932, 85,000 businesses had failed. Nine million savings accounts had been wiped out. The Americans in the city were barely hanging on, and the farmers were going down for the count. President Hoover still found solace in his unshakable belief that somehow the unaided American individual would triumph. The men around him were no more inclined than he to take bold, new initiatives, even as the jobless numbered 15 million.

In places like Sacramento, California, banks urged those who still had jobs to open "good times" bank accounts. The Bank of America ran a cheerful newspaper ad with the phrase "Keep your dollars moving." Deposit money and restore common sense and confidence to the economy, asked the bank. California might just be the state to lead the whole nation back to good times was the hopeful message.[4] The president would have said a hearty "amen" to that. But the sad fact was, not enough people had money to deposit to make a difference anymore.

In May 1932 unemployed veterans who served in World War I had reached the end of their patience. Veterans from all over the country began to talk about marching right up to Herbert Hoover's front door to demand some justice. Their mission would end with violence and just about sound the death knell for President Hoover's hopes of reelection.

4

THE RISE AND FALL
OF THE BONUS ARMY

After World War I a grateful nation granted its war veterans a bonus that was supposed to come due in 1945. But the depression had arrived, and the veterans needed cash. Wasn't it possible for the government to forward some of that bonus money to them right now? In May 1929, Congressman C. Wright Patman introduced a bill in Congress to allow the veterans to borrow money against the bonus. The Bonus Expeditionary Force was marching to Washington to urge passage of the bill.

At the beginning of the march there were 300 veterans with thirty dollars among them. For eighteen days they moved east, many on freight cars and trucks. Veterans from other states heard about the march and decided to enlist. The ranks of the ragtag army swelled. Minnesotans came in boxcars, and 900 men seized trains in Cleveland, Ohio's rail yards to ride them to Washington. By the time the Bonus Army reached the nation's capital, it was 20,000 strong.

These were the doughboys (U.S. Army infantrymen from World War I) who fought in the trenches of France some fourteen years before. These were the boys who'd been bayoneted and gassed who came home with missing limbs or with lungs crippled by poison gas. Times had changed since they'd been welcomed home, when they were hailed with enthusiasm in ticker-tape parades down Fifth Avenue in New York and on Main Streets all over America. Now they had families they couldn't support, and they were hungry, tired, and homeless. They were here from Indiana and Ohio and other states. It had been a long, mean journey of eating bummed sausage and hard bread and living sixty to a boxcar without toilets. It wasn't a lot different from the misery they'd endured in the awful trenches of the western front. But they'd won that war. They were the heroes. How come it hadn't worked out better for heroes? What was the good of being a hero if a man couldn't even feed his own hungry babies? It wasn't right. It wasn't fair. And they were here to tell the president and the Congress that something had to be done about it.

The Bonus Army found shelter in partially razed buildings in Washington left over from World War I. When that space was all used up, the veterans used whatever they could find to make shelters. They lived in egg crates, junked cars, bed frames, and barrels lined up and filled with hay. One veteran could find nothing but an empty coffin, and that became his home. He figured if he didn't get help soon he'd need one of those things, anyway.

The main camp was at Anacostia Flats, right across the Potomac River. The broken-down village came to be called the biggest Hooverville of them all. And the best part was that the veterans could look and see President Hoover's big house from the holes in their egg crates. "Let him forget us now," said one bitter young man. "Let him try not to see us *here.*"

President Hoover did grieve for the needy veterans who confronted him. But he just couldn't see his way clear to give them what they wanted. The government couldn't afford it, he said. It was as simple and sad as that. The secretary of the treasury, Andrew Mellon, warned Hoover that any money advanced to the veterans would unbalance the budget. Mellon believed that if the government spent more than it took in and didn't have a balanced budget, the financial health of the country could be further threatened. A bitter Congressman Patman grumbled, "There are two governments—one run by the elected people—which is a minor part, and one run by the moneyed interests, which controls everything."

On June 15, 1932, the House of Representatives passed the Patman bill, but it never passed the Senate and President Hoover. The country was already reeling from the depression, they said, and so the veterans were reluctantly turned down. Congress decided to give each veteran enough money to get home on the understanding that when the bonus matured, the veterans could pay the government back. It was going to cost the government about a hundred thousand dollars to get the veterans out of Washington.

Some of the veterans folded up their tents and headed home immediately. But many did not. They hadn't come all this way just to take no for an answer. Some of them set up soapboxes and made angry speeches. Others cheered the speeches until they had no voices left. A few visited on the hill with sympathetic congressmen.

In June and July 1932, the remaining veterans were mostly quiet. But discontent was growing, and agitators were joining their ranks. The veterans only wanted a little cash to help them get by, but the Communists who now arrived had bigger fish to fry. They saw the Bonus Army encampment as fertile ground for some revolutionary rabble-rousing.

"Why not try a real revolution?" they whispered in the ears of the veterans. The Communists believed it was only a matter of time before the economic misery in America would lead to a Communist revolution, anyway. Why not now? Why not here? After all, that's how it began in Russia: desperate mobs attacking police stations and looting, cries for bread, and finally—revolution. One Communist agitator who was present among the Bonus Army, John Pace, later admitted that he and his comrades hoped for a real riot as one of the first acts in the American Communist revolution. And President Hoover feared just such an outcome. In a public statement on July 28, he said that the Communists and criminals had taken over the Bonus Army.

The District of Columbia police decided it was time to get the veterans out of the public buildings where they still encamped. At 11:50 A.M. on July 28 the police evacuated about two hundred veterans without serious incident.

"It was a humiliating defeat for our cause," said some angry, embittered veterans.

"Are you going to take it lying down?" asked an agitator. Tempers flared. Just after noon about fifty veterans carrying an American flag attacked a group of police. The police were caught in a savage rain of bricks. The piles of bricks from the ruined buildings provided an excellent source of ammunition. The veterans also threw pieces of lumber, scraps of iron, and anything else they could pry loose. The police responded with billy clubs, and many heads were smartly thumped. Less than two hours later, blood would be shed. Nobody really knows just what happened, how some veterans came to confront police inside a deserted building. The veterans cursed and threatened, and the police felt their lives were in danger. Did the firing begin accidentally when a police officer stumbled? It isn't clearly known, but one veteran fell dead of gunshot wounds, and another was taken away, fatally injured. Three police officers were injured, too.

President Hoover decided that things had gone too far and the veterans must be cleared out at once. Secretary of War Patrick J. Hurley gave the order: U.S. troops proceed immediately to the scene of disorder. Surround the affected area and clear it without delay. Use all humanity consistent with the execution of this order.

To command the evacuation would be Army Chief of Staff General Douglas MacArthur, a forty-eight-year-old hero with years of distinguished service in the Philippines and other Far Eastern nations. When America entered World War I, MacArthur organized the famous "Rainbow" Division, the Forty-second, the first U.S. combat soldiers to arrive in France, made up of soldiers from twenty-six states. Now in the summer of 1932, MacArthur had to move against veterans whose only crime was that they were poor and desperate. It was an unenviable duty for a great soldier, but he did it.

General MacArthur was given five hundred to a thousand soldiers and five tanks to do the job. The soldiers donned gas masks at about 5:30 P.M., and then the encampment was bombed with tear gas. It was an ugly sight—American soldiers in full battle dress arrayed against ragged veterans. One black veteran, carrying the U.S. flag, protested as he was being prodded along by the soldiers, "I fought for this flag! Don't push me!" Although there were a lot of swinging cavalry sabers and menacing thrusts of bayonets, no shots were fired. The Bonus Army was in full retreat. Many escaped into the Maryland woods. By 9:00 P.M. on the night of July 28, the veterans had fled. Their camps were burned; the Washington night sky turned scarlet with the flames of burning wood and canvas. A few remaining veterans and their families watched in stunned sadness. The Bonus Expeditionary

Force had suffered total defeat. President Hoover breathed a sigh of relief and said, "Thank God we still have a government that knows how to deal with a mob."

But a shocked and angry nation looked at pictures of wretched, tattered veterans being cowed by armed men. One news photo showed a veteran clutching an American flag being forced down to the ground and the flag itself being ground under. For millions of depression-weary Americans, the Bonus Army tragedy was the last straw. The year 1932 was an election year, and many made up their minds not to vote for Mr. Hoover in November.

5

THE MARCH TO VICTORY

On June 14, 1932, the less than enthusiastic Republican party convened in Chicago to choose a presidential candidate. There was a funereal atmosphere about the convention. Most everything pointed to the fact that they were only going through the motions. They would be nominating a man with little hope of victory. Herbert Hoover was renominated on the first ballot, and would be the standard-bearer. The only alternative to choosing Hoover would have been to reject the president and all his policies and strike out in a totally different direction. A political party doesn't do this to a sitting president. So the delegates grimly chose their doomed team captain, and in brave, hollow speeches they tried to blame the depression on outside forces. "Hoover was doing the best any president could do against a fierce foe," they argued. And Hoover went forth to campaign like a man with both hands tied behind his back assigned the task of defeating the heavyweight champion.

On the Democrats' side, there was confidence that whoever they nominated at their Chicago convention would become the next president of the United States.

The convention opened on June 27 with many aspirants. Though no Republican was clamoring to ride the elephant this year, many Democrats were all too eager to climb on the donkey's back. Alfred E. Smith, the Catholic former governor of New York who'd been the Democratic candidate for president in 1928, wanted to run again. He was soundly beaten before by Hoover, partially because he was the first Roman Catholic to try for the presidency from a major party. Much anti-Catholic feeling was roused— there were even dark suggestions that if Smith won the White House the Pope would immediately construct a tunnel under the Atlantic Ocean, the better to come over and run the country. When Smith lost the 1928 election, he said wryly, "I told the Pope to stop building the tunnel!" In 1932, however, Smith was the top contender. His supporters thought four years of hard times had made the American people more tolerant.

John Nance Garner of Texas wanted the job, too, as did Democrats from Ohio and Maryland. But the current governor of New York, Franklin Delano Roosevelt, was the biggest threat to the hopes of all the others.

Roosevelt was born January 30, 1882, in Hyde Park, New York. He was the spoiled and only child of rich parents, pampered by a possessive mother and taught by expensive tutors. Roosevelt led a charmed life, making frequent trips to Europe. At age fourteen he went to the fashionable Groton School, then to Harvard. Young Franklin was more interested in social than intellectual pursuits and seemed to be a lightweight. He went to Columbia Law School, and at the age of twenty-three he married his distant cousin Eleanor Roosevelt. Eleanor's uncle, then President Theodore Roosevelt, gave her away in marriage. In 1910, Franklin entered politics, having been elected to the New York State Senate. Then he was appointed assistant secretary of the navy in 1913. Roosevelt didn't impress very many people—he was considered too handsome, too dashing. They took his initials F.D. and nicknamed him Feather Duster Roosevelt.

Then, in 1921, Franklin Roosevelt was stricken by a type of polio called infantile paralysis, an infectious disease that affects the spinal cord. He almost died, and after a terrible struggle with the illness Roosevelt was left paralyzed and unable to walk. For the next two years he swam in the hot mineral waters of Warm Springs, Georgia, and went through exhaustive physical therapy. He once said, "If you have spent two years in bed trying to wiggle your big toe, everything else seems easy."

Despite all the struggle and therapy, Roosevelt would be left seriously physically challenged. He would always be unable to walk without leg braces, a cane, and a strong arm to lean on. Roosevelt came away from the painful experience a different person. He was more serious and compassionate, and he went on to be elected governor of New York in 1928. Now he aspired to the presidency of the United States.

Roosevelt's shrewd campaign manager, James Farley, began to build support for his man at the convention. He had already gathered in most of the delegates from the South and West behind Roosevelt, but they still lacked the two-thirds necessary to win the nomination. Al Smith, with his northern support, tried to join with other hopefuls to stop the Roosevelt drive. Then Farley approached John Nance Garner, who was strong in California and Texas.

"Look," Farley said, "if you swing California and Texas our way, we'll be mighty grateful, John." Garner did just that. Franklin Roosevelt won on the fourth ballot, and who else but "Cactus Jack" Garner was given the vice-presidential position? The Democrats had their ticket, and Roosevelt flew in to accept the nomination. In his acceptance speech he said, "I pledge you, I pledge myself to a New Deal for the American people." The term *New Deal* was used by a Roosevelt speech writer who didn't realize the significance the phrase would take on. From the moment Roosevelt spoke the words, the New Deal became his trademark.

Hoover's managers tried desperately through the summer of 1932 to reverse the damage that years of the depression had done to his image. He was widely considered an uncaring man, stoic in the face of vast suffering. Now they tried to show a shy, but kindly man, the sailor in a storm-tossed ship who had done his best against terrible odds. He was described as a brilliant engineer whose genius would slowly but surely fix everything if the American voter would only trust him a bit longer. Hoover campaigned gallantly in a cause even he suspected was lost. "I have battled on a thousand fronts," Hoover pleaded. "I have fought the good fight to protect our people from hunger and cold."

President Hoover warned that if the Democratic candidate won, grass would grow "in the streets of a hundred cities, a thousand towns." A gloomy Hoover predicted that any change in his policies would "bring disaster to every fireside in America."

On the other hand, Roosevelt's campaign promised something for everybody. In Kansas, Roosevelt assured farmers they'd get relief from rock-bottom prices. In Oregon he promised huge federal hydroelectric projects. To Americans who had lost their life savings on flimflam stock schemes, he promised strict control of the stock exchange. To the unemployed he pledged that nobody would starve and somehow there would be work for willing hands to do.

The conservative banking community was still Republican in 1932, but when President Hoover called Bank of

America's A. P. Giannini asking for assurance of his support, the banker said he didn't get involved with politics. Then, secretly, Giannini wired congratulations to Roosevelt's campaign. With a broad, reassuring smile and a silvery voice, the handsome fifty-year-old governor was winning over even California bankers and many more as well.[1]

Roosevelt could just as easily have spent much of his campaign relying on the use of his superb voice in a radio campaign, which would have been understandable considering his physical handicap, but he refused to do this. He wanted to demonstrate to the American people that he was strong enough, despite his disability, to provide vigorous leadership for the nation. So he conducted an old-fashioned stumping tour of almost every state in the union. He traveled 25,000 miles and talked everywhere of his New Deal for the "forgotten man." It caught on because many Americans felt as if they had been forgotten during those years of misery.

Other, more radical voices were being heard in 1932. The Reverend Charles Coughlin, who ran a nationwide radio program in which he had been railing against bankers and demanding nationalization of all industry, jumped on Roosevelt's bandwagon. "Roosevelt or ruin," cried the burly, smooth-faced priest with the persuasive voice. "The New Deal is Christ's deal!" Huey Long, Louisiana's flamboyant governor, who had a "Share the Wealth" plan of his own to revive the American economy, lined up behind Roosevelt, too. But William Z. Foster, presidential candidate of the American Communist party, attacked Roosevelt and shouted slogans like "Workers of the world unite, you have nothing to lose but your chains." Foster recalled the words of Joseph Stalin, despotic ruler of the Soviet Union, who said, "I think the moment is not far off when a revolutionary crisis will develop in America." The Communist party stood ready to make the most of such a crisis. Norman Thomas, the Socialist candidate, also rejected the New Deal and asked America to junk capitalism for socialism.

On the right wing of politics, many businessmen feared Roosevelt would lead America on a downhill slide if elected. Conservative Congressman Hamilton Fish claimed Roosevelt was "a Socialist, or worse."[2] From the far left-wingers who accused Roosevelt of not going far enough in making economic reforms part of his program to the far right-wingers who charged he would undermine capitalism, the criticism was fierce. Many wondered just what political philosophy Franklin Roosevelt did follow. In an anecdote later related by cabinet officer Frances Perkins, an answer could be found.

A newspaper reporter had asked Roosevelt, "Are you a Communist?" Roosevelt replied, "No." The answer was the same when Roosevelt was asked if he was a capitalist or a socialist. Roosevelt then simply stated what his philosophy was. He was, he said, "A Christian and a Democrat."[3]

Roosevelt's religious beliefs profoundly affected his character and how he saw the world and his role in it. He believed in a personal God, an absolute ethic of right and wrong, and in the essential goodness of his fellow human beings. His strong belief in a government that should help people in dire need convinced Roosevelt that the president must be instrumental in making decency, justice, and fair play triumph.

Will Rogers described the mood of many voters as election day dawned. "The little fellow felt that he never had a chance and he 'dident' till November the 8th. And did he grab it!"

On election day, Roosevelt polled 57.3 percent of all votes cast. He won 472 electoral votes. Hoover polled 39.6 percent of the vote, winning only the 59 electoral votes of the New England states and Delaware. Norman Thomas, the socialist, got close to a million votes, but William Z. Foster, who believed America was ripe for Communist revolution, got a paltry 100,000 votes.

Victory had been won, but at Roosevelt's celebration dinner jubilation gave way to a realization of the monumental task ahead. Complicating matters was that the president-elect wouldn't be inaugurated until March 4 of the following year. This meant that for almost four months, America would have a new but powerless president and an old president who could do even less than he had done before. (To correct this problem in future elections, the Twentieth Amendment was ratified in 1933 providing for the newly elected president to take office on the twentieth day of January.)

The exhausted and rejected Hoover now had to run the ship of state during weeks of great crisis. Many called this period in American history the most dangerous time since the Civil War. The financial structure of America was on the brink of catastrophe. The very foundations of American capitalism seemed about to crumble like a stone building in an earthquake. By January 1933, rumors of massive bank failures fueled rising panic. Small investors hurried to rescue their life savings, only to find that the banks had already closed. Luckier ones found their banks still open, but as they transferred their money from bank vaults to home mattresses, even the solvent banks became shaky. In October 1932 the governor of Nevada closed the banks for twelve days to head off a wild run that would have destroyed every bank in the state. One string of Nevada banks foreclosed (took possession of because the mortgage could no longer be paid by the owners) on 150 ranches that owned 70 percent of all the cattle and sheep in the state. The state's economy had deteriorated to the extent that the banks had to sell the sheep for twenty-five cents a head though they had loaned eight dollars a head on the same herds.

In February 1933, the governor of Louisiana closed the banks in that state. Not long after, the state of Michigan followed suit. State after state fell like pins in a bowling alley, leading almost all Americans to lose all confidence in the safety of bank accounts.

During these four months before he could take office, Roosevelt was not standing still by any means. He was preparing for the time when he could take over. Roosevelt was assembling his cabinet and creating an inner circle of advisers called the "Brain Trust." This group included university professors and lawyers. Raymond Moley was an expert on public law and Rexford G. Tugwell was an economist. They and others wrote speeches, prepared public statements, and planned how they would carry out New Deal policies.

It seemed to most Americans that March 4 would never come, so impatient was the nation for new leadership. Then, at last, on a gloomy, rainy Saturday that matched the mood of the nation, the new president was sworn in.

One hundred thousand men, women, and children were gathered at the inauguration platform on the east front of the Capitol as the car carrying Roosevelt and Hoover arrived. People covered forty acres of park and pavement. Some sat in trees, on benches, and even on rooftops. The bugle sounded, and Franklin Roosevelt appeared, leaning on the arm of his son, James. He shuffled slowly down a maroon carpeted ramp while the band played "Hail to the Chief." Without an overcoat or hat in the chilly, misty day, the new president began his speech. Unsmiling, he would speak for about twenty minutes.

"My friends," the president began, "this is a day of national consecration. The only thing we have to fear is fear itself—nameless, unreasoning, unjustified terror which paralyzes needed efforts to convert retreat into advance."

The president's speech, carried on the radio, brought no less than 460,000 letters pouring into the White House. The New Deal was at last under way, and Americans were hoping against hope that now, finally, the horrendous problems of the economy would be tackled.

To get an idea of how far America had fallen by 1933, statistics such as the following might be examined: In 1929, 4,600,000 cars were sold, while barely a million were sold in 1932. Five hundred thousand new homes were built in 1929, compared to 100,000 in 1932. Those dismal figures reflect the lost jobs of all the auto workers, carpenters, plumbers, stone masons, and other skilled people who would have made the cars and houses never built. The sale of durable consumer goods like washing machines and stoves had dropped by half. Per capita income in 1929 was $681; by 1933 it had fallen to $495. Most working women in Chicago—those who were lucky enough to have work at all—earned five to ten dollars a week. A fourth of America's working women earned less than ten cents an hour. A first-class New York stenographer who earned $35 to $45 a week in 1929 was now lucky to draw $16 a week, while domestic workers barely made $10 a month plus room and board.

In New York City, Mayor Fiorello La Guardia was serving as city magistrate when a man was brought before him for the crime of stealing a loaf of bread for his starving family. La Guardia said, "I must fine you ten dollars," but then the mayor paid the fine himself and said, "I hereby fine every person in this courtroom, except for the prisoner, fifty cents for living in a town where a man has to steal in order to eat." The mayor gave the $47.50 in fines to the prisoner. [4]

As Franklin Roosevelt took the reins of power under these terrible circumstances, the American people came to know his wife, Eleanor, about as well as they knew him. No retiring housewife, not content to devote her energies to preparing state dinners, Anna Eleanor Roosevelt would be unique among American first ladies.

Anna Eleanor Roosevelt was born in New York City on October 11, 1884. When she lost both her parents at a young age, she went to live with her grandmother. A lonely and awkward child, educated in the United States and England, she developed an early sympathy for the poor and less privileged. It was Eleanor who took her young husband, Franklin, to see the awful slums of New York, introducing him to a side of life he'd been shielded from before. During the 1920s, Eleanor established the Val-Kill Furniture Shop in Hyde Park for unemployed people. She also taught at the Rivington Street Settlement House (for poor children) and started the Todhunter School for girls, where she continued to teach even after her husband became governor of New York. Franklin Roosevelt credited his wife's strength in helping him through his paralyzing illness and encouraging him to seek higher office.

Tall, thin, and energetic, Eleanor was always a strong person in her own right. She plunged at once into the problems of the depression. She had been Franklin's eyes and ears while he was governor, going to places where her husband's disability made it difficult for him to visit. She continued this as the first lady, traveling 40,000 miles the first year Roosevelt was president. She took firsthand looks at the conditions of migrant workers, coal miners, and the unemployed in the cities. She talked to people in soup lines and municipal kitchens. She was especially interested in young people. With five children of her own, she had a way of making dispirited, youthful victims of the depression feel that she was sincerely interested in them.

Once, Eleanor Roosevelt entered a home where the family slept on the floor in dirty sacking. In one corner a small child fearfully clutched a pet rabbit, certain the need to eat it soon would arise. In another home the president's wife met a young woman living in deep poverty who kept up her courage by clipping out magazine pictures of nice homes, making of them a collage of some future "house of dreams." Mrs. Roosevelt carried such stories back to her husband, constantly urging him to greater efforts to keep such dreams alive.

Mrs. Roosevelt had her critics. Some people thought she wielded too much influence. Her ideas seemed to be to the left of her husband's, and some Americans grew to hate and fear her. Still, few denied that she provided a valuable link between her husband and the American people during the difficult days of the depression.

As Franklin Roosevelt began to lead America, the order of business at hand was to solve the banking crisis. During what would be called "the first one hundred days," Roosevelt lost no time in dealing with the financial disaster that was at the doorstep.

6

THE FIRST
"HUNDRED DAYS"—
PART ONE

Two days after he was inaugurated, on March 6, 1933, Roosevelt ordered a bank holiday. All American banks were ordered to close for four days. Congress then met in special session and in just four hours enacted the first of what would be a long series of legislative responses to the depression. So many banks had failed as a result of unwise and even dishonest banking practices that the government was now going to regulate all banking procedures.

The Emergency Banking Act was the first of the New Deal measures in what would be a momentous 100 days of almost frenzied lawmaking. This bill provided for the reopening of the banks under a tight system of licenses and conservators. It also gave the U.S. Treasury the power to issue more currency and prevent the hoarding of gold. Government supervision of banks would include making sure that banks did not make unsound loans that were unlikely to be paid back. Government inspectors would regularly examine the bank's books to see if each loan made had a reasonable chance of being repaid. For example, if the bank loaned someone money to buy a house, they had to insist that the debtor had at least some of his own money to make the down payment. With his own money involved, the mortgage payer was less likely to walk away from his obligations and leave the bank holding the bag. By demanding that Americans return hoarded gold, the government was preventing the dangerous belief from taking root that government-issued money was no good and you could only trust a lump of gold.

On March 12, 1933, President Roosevelt conducted the first fireside chat, a radio address to the American people. It was a new, dramatic way for a president to communicate directly to the people, and it proved to be a powerful link to the American public. By 1933 the radio enjoyed a dominant role in American life, with several popular shows broadcast to almost every home. So when Roosevelt's soothing voice came on, everybody listened attentively. That voice in the living room seemed to speak to each American individually. So when the president promised that the banks that would be allowed to reopen would be safe places for money, it sounded believable. He explained simply what the government was doing and asked the people to trust him. He was taking the entire nation into his confidence and making them believe we were all in this together and by working together no problem was too big to be solved.

The response of the people was swift and heartwarming to the president. By the first week in April, more than a billion dollars in currency had returned to reopened banks. People who had been hoarding gold brought it in in exchange for the currency they felt they could trust again. The fear that the entire American banking system was about to collapse faded. The mass of small depositors could now feel confidence again. In two weeks President Roosevelt had driven back the fear enveloping the nation. Ninety percent of the banks reopened soundly, and the rest were declared insolvent and permanently closed. The actions of the president were hailed as swift and decisive even by some of his critics. Will Rogers said, "America hasn't been as happy in three years as [it is] today." A woman in New England said, "We feel that our country has been given back to us."

Now the president turned to a bill that would make sure that never again would Americans have to worry about money in the bank. In June 1933, the Glass-Steagall Banking Act was passed. It created the Federal Deposit Insurance Corporation (FDIC) to guarantee that the first $5,000 anybody deposited in the bank would be guaranteed by the government. Even if the bank folded, the government would return every penny in the account to the depositor. It was iron-clad security for American savers. The amount guaranteed was gradually increased, but in 1933, $5,000 was adequate for most savings accounts. Millions of people had seen their small accounts of several hundred or a couple thousand dollars swept away as banks folded. Now the president assured them that it would never happen again. Generations of Americans would never put money in an account again without pausing at the door to check for the FDIC sign.

Other provisions of the Glass-Steagall bill reformed corruption in the banking system. These were the result of an inquiry by Judge Ferdinand Pecora. Born in Nicosia, Sicily, Pecora was a former New York district attorney. He conducted a sensational investigation in which he questioned such titans of business as J. P. Morgan. In the process he discovered a sordid tale of wild financial speculation that had endangered the nation. Banks invested savers' money in shaky stocks. They loaned huge amounts of money to businesses without investigating the background of the people involved. Any smooth-talking con man could expect to get a huge loan at the bank even if he already had a trail of unpaid debts in his past. Under the new rules, banks were forced out of the stock market-investing business and forbidden to undertake land-speculation schemes in which chances for success were limited. In short, the banks would no longer be allowed to be wild gamblers with other peoples' money.

In March 1933, Congress passed the Economy Act. All federal employees took a 15 percent salary cut. The act was so unpopular that the cuts were quickly restored. More successful was the Truth in Securities Act to protect the public from fraud in the issuance of stocks and other securities. High-powered salesmen could no longer prey on naive buyers without risking the wrath of the Federal Trade Commission (FTC).

Still in March, the president personally came up with one of his most important New Deal programs. It was designed to conserve both human and natural resources. The Civilian Conservation Corps (CCC) was created in late March, and it enrolled 250,000 young men from families on relief. The men, between the ages of eighteen and twenty-five who were in need and capable of doing hard work, received room and board and $30 per month. Of this amount, $25 was sent to the young men's families, and the men kept $5 for spending money. The youths of the CCC were sent to work camps that were originally built by the War Department for military camps. Once set up in about fifteen hundred camps, they built dams, roads, drained marshes to control mosquitoes, and planted 17 million acres of new forests.

For many of the young men at the CCC camps it was their first time away from home. Before settling into the routine, they didn't receive the kind of training military recruits get. All sorts of youth were thrown together, and they had various attitudes toward hygiene. Some of the lads who didn't believe in bathing regularly were soon taught by their companions that those who didn't wash would risk getting a harsh scrubbing with hard-bristled brushes from fellow campers. But generally the CCC men got along well, and the program gave them something they'd never had before—a chance to do useful work and help their families at the same time. Besides, they had a few dollars to spend as they wished, and in 1933, $5 was often more than family heads had to spend on their own needs.

In April 1933, Roosevelt took America off the gold standard. By 1914, gold was the measuring stick for all the currencies of the world. By having this one standard of value, it was easier for nations to trade with one another. The American dollar, the French franc, and the German mark all had a set value in gold. For example, one ounce of gold might equal in value four marks, three francs, and two dollars. So if you bought an item whose real value was one ounce of gold, you could pay for it in marks, francs, or dollars and be paying the same price.

Having this set value enabled nations to trade with one another. Otherwise, nobody would quite know if six francs was more or less than six dollars. Paper currency was used, not gold, but it was backed by a pile of gold somewhere in the country. In the United States, bars of gold were stored at Fort Knox, Kentucky. This stored gold was called a reserve, and every government bond or bill over $20 could be exchanged for actual gold. The government guaranteed this until we went off the gold standard. Most other nations had lifted the gold standard earlier, so their money was more plentiful and cheaper. If you cannot print more than $20 without having a lump of gold sitting somewhere, your ability to print a lot of money is limited. Therefore, your money is scarce and more costly. American products were more expensive and harder to sell on the world market because our money was tied to having a fixed amount of gold. When we went off the gold standard and didn't have to back up every dollar with a specified lump of gold, our ability to sell products improved. Some denounced the move as "the end of Western civilization," but Roosevelt did cause a small surge in the economy by his move. Even today, gold is used as a general basis for judging the value of currency, but the strict limiting of currency to the actual existence of a certain amount of gold bars has ended.

In May 1933, the Federal Emergency Relief Act was passed. Roosevelt was now doing what Hoover had found impossible—he gave direct relief to people in need. Six million people were on city and state relief rolls, and another fifteen million were out of work and surviving with the help of relatives and friends as well as an occasional part-time job. Five hundred million dollars was immediately allocated for these people.

Responding to severe economic distress in the agricultural sector, the Emergency Farm Mortgage Act was also passed in May 1933. Farm foreclosures had become the nightmare of rural America, with some farms worth $80,000 being sold at auction for a $15,000 mortgage. President Roosevelt's new act halted foreclosures and enabled farmers to refinance their mortgages so they would be easier to pay off.

But the Emergency Farm Mortgage Act did not address the basic sickness that afflicted America's farms. The times clamored for a more important program, which the president would also carry out during the first 100 days.

7

THE FIRST
"HUNDRED DAYS"—
PART TWO

A Minnesota farmer wrote a letter to Eleanor Roosevelt. Scrawled on cheap scratch paper he wrote, "I am trying to hold my farm and get food for my children, but it is hard this year. Money is scarce and hard to get." Mrs. Roosevelt took the letter to her husband, who wrote back, "All I ask is that you believe we are honestly trying to do our best and we think we are slowly but surely improving conditions."

In 1933 it seemed that even nature had turned against the farmer. Dust storms, droughts, floods, and grasshopper plagues were widespread. Decades of soil depletion in the Great Plains from Texas to Canada were taking their toll. On November 11, 1933, a black blizzard was under way— a violent dust storm that blew away much of the fertile topsoil in the Dakotas, Kansas, and Oklahoma. Houses, trees, and machinery were blanketed with dirt. The sun seemed to go out in the middle of the day as yellowish brown clouds rolled endlessly across the land. Many stricken farmers abandoned their homesteads and piled in broken-down jalopies to head for California.

But in May 1933, just about 60 days into the first "hundred days," the Agricultural Adjustment Act (AAA) was passed. Roosevelt tried by this law to raise farm incomes back to where they were the last time American farmers enjoyed a decent standard of living—way back in 1914. To carry out the policies of the AAA, Roosevelt chose Henry A. Wallace as secretary of agriculture. A profarmer crusader, the 45-year-old shock-haired Wallace came from a respected agricultural family that produced the highly respected farm journal *Wallace's Farmer.*

The AAA was designed to maintain a balance between production and consumption of commodities. In other words, production had to be controlled. Farmers could no longer produce as much as they could of anything without the market justifying it. Farm income would remain stable only if there were buyers for most of the peanuts and potatoes that were on the market. This was the supply-and-demand principle—that is, if the supply of anything (from tophats to tomatoes) is greater than the demand, prices go down. If the demand is greater than the supply, prices go up. So the AAA authorized the Department of Agriculture to send county agents in every state out to the farms to check on what was being produced.

The agents inspected commodities like grain, cotton, tobacco, peanuts, and sugar. If there was not a demand for more than five million acres of cotton, not an acre more could be planted. In some cases, the agents found too many acres already planted with cotton. Cotton farmers were paid $200 million to plow under ten million acres of cotton—a third of the cotton crop. Meat producers were ordered to cut production of pigs and cattle because there were already too many heads of cattle and pigs on the market. Six million piglets were already born in excess of the total number of piglets the government wanted. These had to be slaughtered and kept off the market. Hog prices had plummeted dramatically. They were now worth four to five cents a pound, far less than it had cost to raise them. Cotton was down to four cents a pound, though it cost ten cents to produce that pound.

Cattle and even oranges had to be destroyed to try to reduce supply and to raise prices. Dorothy Comingore, a California actress, recalled: "I saw heaps of oranges covered with gasoline and set on fire and men who tried to steal one orange were shot."[1] In no piece of literature was the bitterness of needy people seeing crops destroyed portrayed so powerfully as in John Steinbeck's book *The Grapes of Wrath.* Steinbeck wrote, "The works of the roots, of the vines, of the trees must be destroyed to keep up the price, and this is the saddest, bitterest thing of all. A million people hungry, needing the fruit and kerosene sprayed on the golden mountains and the smell of rot fills the country."[2]

Opponents of the AAA violently attacked Wallace and Roosevelt for all this. The spectacle of wanton destruction of food as a hungry nation went without seemed insane. The destruction of millions of fields of cotton in an ill-clad nation seemed wicked. One critic said that it proved mules were smarter than people in government. But the critics didn't mention that the slaughtered piglets were turned into frozen pork to be given to hungry people through the Federal Surplus Relief Corporation. Nor did the critics really seem to know how desperate President Roosevelt was in the summer of 1933. He had given the War Department orders to prepare rolling kitchens to feed needy people around the nation. He feared that in spite of all the millions the federal government was spending, winter could well be a starving time for the nation. He wasn't worrying needlessly. In some rural areas, families had eaten off the barks of trees and dinner was a dish of wild dandelions.

For all the criticism directed against the AAA, it did answer the three main demands of farmers. They wanted higher prices for their crops, the chance to refinance loans over a longer period, and cash relief to pay debts. Farm prices did begin to rise. Wheat was 38¢ a bushel in 1932 and by 1936 it was $1.02. Loans were refinanced, and farmers received cash payments for crops they didn't plant. These they used to pay debts. Many farm families found their heads above water for the first time in many years.

In May 1933, President Roosevelt also launched another program, both dramatic and controversial. The Tennessee Valley Authority (TVA) Act created a corporation with three directors appointed by the president. They had the power to build dams and power plants for the welfare of the people in the Tennessee River Valley.

The TVA idea was sold to President Roosevelt by Nebraska Senator George Norris. Norris was born in Ohio of poor parents. He lost his father at age four, and his elder brother died in the Civil War. While still a teenager, Norris helped hack out a living for his mother and many sisters on a stump-covered Ohio farmland. Norris said, "Only those who've lived on a farm know the agony of cycles of crop failures and debts." He believed it was the duty of government to "make use of the earth for the good of man."

Norris convinced the president that the well-being of millions of Americans would be achieved by the TVA. A mighty river that often wrought horrendous damage would be brought under control, the fertility of the land would be restored, and eroded farms could produce again. There would be cheaper electricity, and the living conditions of the people would be vastly improved in the valley.

But should the whole nation's taxes be used for the benefit of just one region in so large a scheme? Congress and the president said yes! So 40,000 men were hired to form a construction team to do what one carpenter called "one hell of a big job of work." Twenty new dams were built, and existing ones were improved. Dams with names like Pickwick Landing, Wolf Creek, and Hiwassee came on line. Two and one-half times the concrete used in the whole Panama Canal was poured by the TVA.

In the end the project would cost $2 billion, but it was perfect for what it was designed to do. In an area where annual rainfall is extremely heavy, there were no more floods. Once the dams were completed, there was an inland waterway 652 miles long connecting the South with the Great Lakes and the Ohio and Missouri and Mississippi River system. Barges could now bring automobiles from Detroit and steel from Chicago right into the Deep South.

And there were other benefits of TVA, too. Youth from the CCC learned how to prevent soil erosion and rebuild the land. They planted trees and developed a demonstration program to teach farmers all over the country to do the same. Cash from farming in the Tennessee River valley jumped 200 percent.

The TVA eventually became a major producer of electric power in the United States, but that created problems. Private utility companies cried "foul" and "unfair competition" because a tax-supported agency was underselling them. Years of court battles followed before the TVA was free of litigation. But the TVA had provided an important blueprint for the future: government could undertake huge public programs to improve the life of a region and reverse centuries of environmental damage.

In June 1933, Congress passed the Home Owners' Loan Corporation (HOLC) Act, which did for private homeowners in cities and towns what the Emergency Farm Mortgage Act had done for farmers. It helped struggling homeowners who were facing foreclosure on their homes; 300,000 federally guaranteed loans were given to these people in one year. With federally refinanced loans that they could pay off over a longer period at lower monthly payments, eventually about a million people kept homes that would otherwise have been taken from them.

Toward the end of the incredible first "100 days" of lawmaking, President Roosevelt designed yet another program that he hoped would be the "silver bullet" that would finally turn the corner and put America on the mend. It was the National Industrial Recovery Act (NIRA), which set up the National Recovery Administration (NRA), whose symbol was a big blue eagle clutching a cogwheel in its claws.

The man in charge of the NRA would be General Hugh "Ironpants" Johnson, an old cavalryman with a hard, leathery face, squinty eyes, and a quick temper. Johnson was a West Pointer determined to run "this thing" like a war campaign. He warned, "May God Almighty have mercy on anyone who attempts to trifle with that bird—the blue eagle!"

Roosevelt truly believed he had something big with the NRA. "History," he said, "will record the National Industrial Recovery Act as the most important and far reaching legislation ever enacted by the American Congress. It represents a supreme effort to stabilize for all times the many factors which make for the prosperity of the nation and the preservation of American standards."

But the president was much too optimistic about his new brainchild. The NRA would turn out to be as popular with the business sector as an army of ants at a picnic. Basically, the NRA would try to restore the health of the American economy by drafting codes for every industry. These codes would encourage collective bargaining between labor and industry—that is, employers negotiating with groups of workers formed into unions, not with individual workers—to decide such things as wages and working conditions. The NRA set up maximum work hours beyond which people were not allowed to work—for instance, an employee could not be expected to put in twelve hours. Also, a minimum wage for workers was established. Offering someone wages below this minimum was illegal. Section 7A promised a living wage for labor and a reasonable profit for business. In all, the National Recovery Administration drafted 746 different codes to apply to various industries.

In the past, the government had opposed industry practices called monopolizing. This meant companies would all agree on one price for an item. The government argued that this was unfair to consumers because they couldn't shop around and find cheaper products. Now, under the NRA, the government itself was sponsoring monopolistic price fixing. For example, the price of a gallon of milk would be set at ten cents. No milk producer could sell it for nine cents even if he could do so and make a profit. The NRA bureaucrats said that dropping the price would undercut competitors and threaten the milk industry.

Similarly, business output was carefully controlled. Government told every business how much they could make of everything. If the Spiral Clock Works Company was told to produce 500 clocks a month, they better not produce 505. Business people bitterly resented this intrusion into their activities.

Advertising was also strictly controlled, and false advertising as well as attacks on the reputation of competitors was forbidden. The ban on false advertising forced businesses not to exaggerate the value of their products. This meant that the Fluffy Mattress Company could neither claim more feathers than actually were in *their* mat-

The Roaring Twenties was a prosperous time. Here, six women turn out in full regalia for a society luncheon picnic in 1926.

Almost anybody could afford a car during the 1920s. This 1925 photograph shows a parking lot packed with Ford Model T Tin Lizzies and other cars, outside Nantasket Beach, Massachusetts.

Anxious people throng the steps of a building across the street from the New York Stock Exchange in October 1929, when thousands of people's life savings were wiped out in a spectacular crash.

President Herbert Hoover, less than a month after Black Thursday dealt a deathblow to Wall Street

Seattle's destitute families lived in shacks during the 1930s. This village, like other makeshift camps for the unemployed, was nicknamed "Hooverville," after President Hoover.

Hunger and despair were the constant companions of
millions of Americans during the depression era.

In 1931, the first subsidized penny restaurant in New York City boasted a menu where each dish sold for one cent and a modest five-course meal could be purchased for a nickel.

Demonstrators gather at Manhattan's Union Square in 1932 to air their grievances about the deplorable economy.

"Buy an apple!" Fred Bell, a millionaire before the Crash in 1929, sold apples for a living at a street corner in San Francisco.

Men wait patiently outside an employment agency in
Manhattan. Over 12 million Americans were unemployed
when Franklin Roosevelt became president.
Facing page: Times Square before and after the Crash:
The depression transformed the well-fed, well-heeled
crowds of Broadway into hungry queues waiting for
a sandwich and a cup of coffee.

(Top) Unable to pay their taxes, Virginia
farmers listen in despair as their land is
being sold at a public auction. Some parcels
of land were sold for as low as thirty cents
per acre. (Bottom) Jobless World War I
veterans on the way to the nation's capital,
where they unsuccessfully lobbied for early
payment of their bonus checks.

Eleanor and Franklin Roosevelt in their home in Hyde Park, New York, in 1928.

A time for change: Roosevelt addresses the 1932 Chicago Democratic Convention.

Members of the Civilian Conservation Corps
(CCC) head for another day's
work in the forest.

The year 1933 brought more headaches for
the farmers. Drought and dust storms forced
thousands of families to abandon their farms on
the Great Plains for the promise of California.

Eager to share his New Deal programs, the president delivers one of his fireside chats to millions of radio listeners.

The First Lady donned an apron and served soup to unemployed women during a visit to New York City.

(Above) The Works Progress Administration (WPA) created over two thousand projects, which were intended to put millions of people back to work. Here, a WPA-sponsored sewing project is under way in Washington, D.C.
(Facing page) The Tennessee Valley Authority (TVA) and the National Recovery Administration (NRA) were among the many agencies created under the New Deal during the Roosevelt administration's first "hundred days." The top photograph shows a dam under construction that would provide flood control and hydroelectric power to the Tennessee River valley. The bottom picture shows the NRA flag, bearing the "blue recovery eagle" that came to symbolize the New Deal.

Architects of the New Deal: (clockwise from top left) Henry A. Wallace, head of the Agricultural Adjustment Act (AAA); George Norris, mastermind of the Tennessee Valley Authority (TVA); Harry "Mr. Root of the Matter" Hopkins, head of the Federal Emergency Relief Association (FERA); and Hugh "Ironpants" Johnson, head of the National Recovery Administration (NRA).

The United States Supreme Court in 1939. Front row, left to right, are associate justices Harlan Fiske Stone and James Clark McReynolds; Chief Justice Charles Evans Hughes; associate justices Pierce Butler and Owen J. Roberts. Back row, left to right, are four of Roosevelt's appointees: associate justices Felix Frankfurter, Hugo L. Black, Stanley F. Reed, and William O. Douglas.

FDR signs into law the Social Security Act
of 1935, which he considered the crowning
achievement of his administration.

tresses nor hint that Comfy Mattresses, put out by the competition, were lumpy.

A controversial code forbade industries to make technical advances that might lead to laying off workers. For example, if a manufacturer had a new machine that enabled a worker to make six shoes per hour instead of two, that machine could not be used. This restriction was ominous for the future of American industry because manufacturers were stuck with horse-and-buggy methods while other nations modernized and produced the same goods cheaper and more efficiently.

Most annoying of all to business people was that the federal government was now peering over their shoulder with truly an "eagle eye." Many Americans were afraid that this threatened American freedoms. A businessman in the Northeast complained, "We are being condemned to the gray mediocrity of government-imposed tyranny." Making matters worse was that the codes were drawn up hastily and some were unduly cumbersome or even ridiculous. They stifled the very creativity that would help America get out of the depression. In Cleveland, Ohio, grocers grumbled that the NIRA was the worst law ever enacted and that the National Recovery Administration it created should be renamed National Run Around.

Still, President Roosevelt enthusiastically charged forward with his big blue bird. Posters bearing the blue eagle appeared in every shop window. The bird showed up on magazine covers and in the movies. Girls dancing in a Broadway chorus line dutifully wore NRA eagles on their costumes. And old "Ironpants" Johnson flew around America in army planes trying to sell the program as the best thing since sliced white bread. A first-class salesman, Johnson pleaded and threatened, shouted and sweet-talked, his listeners. He was determined to sell the NRA even if many believed the eagle was a turkey in disguise. Johnson would do his best to make the thing fly, whatever it was.

Title II of the NIRA established the Public Works Administration (PWA) to build public buildings and roads and offer wages to the unemployed to do the job. Roosevelt put a man named Harold Ickes in charge. The president pictured the summer coming alive with hammering and sawing and the whirr of cement mixers as new hospitals, university buildings, municipal water works, and bridges were built. Three billion, 300 million dollars was set aside for the PWA. But the careful, methodical Ickes was not about to spend a penny unwisely or in haste.

Denounced by Louisiana's Governor Huey Long as "Chinch-bug Ickes" for his penny-pinching ways, Ickes scrutinized and studied every program from all directions. Eventually his caution led to the building of many sound highways and fine projects, but Roosevelt's hopes for quick employment for the suffering millions faded. The PWA was bogged down in a ton of red tape, and the misery of the unemployed went on. The failure of the PWA to accomplish what Roosevelt intended led many angry Americans to wonder if the smiling Roosevelt was much better than the president he had replaced.

Still, the NRA gains included wages rising from $5 a week to $12, the strengthening of labor unions, and better working conditions for many employees. Further down the road, the U.S. Supreme Court would strike down the blue eagle, but for now it flew on.

One of the brightest and most effective of the New Dealers chosen by Roosevelt to dispense relief in those first "hundred days" was Harry L. Hopkins. Hopkins, the son of a midwestern harnessmaker, was called by British statesman Winston Churchill "Mr. Root of the Matter" for his amazing ability to get to the bottom of a problem quickly.

Hopkins shared Roosevelt's desire to rush help to the American people. He was a hard-driving man who hit the ground running when given his marching orders. He was so eager to put the New Deal programs into effect that he refused to wait until his desk was moved into his office before beginning work. He found the desk in the hall amid packing cases, sat down, and went to work. When some-one told Hopkins that a project would work "in the long run," he snapped back, "People don't eat in the long run. They eat every day."

Critics called Hopkins a sloppy administrator because he was impatient with details and eager for action. He wouldn't take the time to write letters. As head of the direct relief program of the New Deal Federal Emergency Relief Association (FERA), he'd learn about a city in Arkansas that had run out of relief money and order "a million dollars to Arkansas tomorrow morning." When he'd find out about New Yorkers trying to survive on salt pork and beans he'd grab the phone and tell the FERA cashiers to "send five million dollars to New York imme-diately." He knew he was holding the lives of human beings in his hands and that delays could not be tolerated.

At the end of the first "hundred days," James A. Farley, Roosevelt's postmaster general marveled, "The president saved our free enterprise system—he saved the banks. What he has done in these first hundred days—this was a tremendous job!"

Unemployment was still high, and the depression was far from beaten, but the degree of human suffering caused by the depression had been significantly decreased by the New Deal programs. President Roosevelt had made a breathtakingly fast start.

8

MINORITIES IN
THE DEPRESSION

Well before the onset of the depression, African-Americans suffered higher unemployment rates than whites. The depression only made this situation worse. By 1933, 25 to 40 percent of black workers were unemployed. In the South, where discriminatory laws were still legal, relief programs did not serve blacks well. In Louisiana they received food filled with worms and weevils. In many areas the same local governments that had provided unequal educational and recreational facilities now provided unequal relief or none at all.

At the beginning of the New Deal, Eleanor Roosevelt reached out in a special way to black Americans. She was a close friend of Mary McLeod Bethune, a prominent African-American educator. As the two women frequently dined together, the president's wife learned of the special problems of black people.

Black Americans had largely voted Republican ever since Abraham Lincoln, the Great Emancipator, had ended slavery. All this was about to change with the advent of the New Deal. President Roosevelt appointed Mary

McLeod Bethune to a major advisory spot in the government. African-Americans appeared at social functions at the White House for the first time.

Horace Clayton, a black sociologist in Chicago described the tense atmosphere in his neighborhood prior to the Roosevelt years: "There were long, angry marches with chanting, shouting people demanding that the government pay attention to their needs. Communist agitators infiltrated the groups, substituting words like Brother Stalin and Father Lenin * for the spiritual references in the old Negro spirituals. But President Roosevelt and his wife brought new hope. People could endure the miserable present if they believed there was something being done to make the future better."

Mexican-Americans in the Southwest shared in the widespread woes of the farm, but they had even less to start with. An Arizona family watched a giant tractor knock down their corrals and buildings, then climbed into an old Chevy truck and headed for California. The young son related how his father grieved over losing the small piece of land he'd owned and always swore he would once again own a farm. The foreclosure left a permanent imprint of sadness on the man's face. He never did fulfill his dream, remaining, with his family, a member of the migrant work force for the rest of his life.

In Indio, California, a Mexican-American family stopped at a small restaurant for coffee. Unable to read English, the father walked past the sign saying "white trade only," but his son behind him read the message. The waitress told the man, "We don't serve Mexicans—get out of here," adding racism to the already heavy burden of poverty the family suffered.

* Joseph Stalin, Communist leader of Russia, and Vladimir Ilyich Ulyanov Lenin, founder of Russian communism.

For Jewish-Americans, the 1930s were also doubly cruel. The economic collapse of 1929 brought on a new wave of anti-Semitism. People often look for scapegoats when things are going badly. Over in Germany, the Nazis spread savage hatred of the Jews, blaming the nation's misery on Jewish bankers. Such bigotry found ready ears in America as well. Hatemongers like the Silver Shirt legion, modeled after Hitler's Brown Shirts, vandalized Jewish-owned businesses. Even an elected representative from Pennsylvania denounced "Jewish money power" from the floor of Congress, and there were some who dubbed the New Deal the "Jew Deal," hinting darkly that Roosevelt himself was a Jew, descended from a colonial family named Rosenvelt that had been expelled from New Amsterdam.

Despite the myth of widespread wealth, Jewish families suffered the same deprivations of other Americans. They could be found in bread lines and soup lines and in sadly declining circumstances. One small Jewish girl watched fearfully as the adults gathered behind locked doors at night to discuss financial problems. Then the furniture began to disappear. When the house was lost, they moved to the apartment of their grandparents. Treats disappeared, and clothing turned shabby, but the father of the family would never admit to his children how terrible their situation was. To admit it was just too much for a once-proud merchant whose years of hard work had come to nothing.

Chinese-Americans, already often persecuted by their neighbors in good times, seemed to fare much better during the depression. White Americans gave them their grudging admiration as the tightly knit Chinese communities cared for their own in mutual-aid societies.

The American Indian, far down the ladder of prosperity in all times, also received a New Deal from the administration of President Roosevelt. John Collier was appointed commissioner of Indian affairs; he had a genuine sympathy for the Indians.

Prior to this, Indians lived under the old Dawes Act. Life on the reservations shockingly became filled with poverty and disease, as the Indians had one of the lowest life-expectancy rates in the country. Indians were not allowed to make decisions affecting their own lives. The government had an allotment plan by which heads of families could buy 160 acres of land and begin life as private farmers, not as members of their tribe. It was not successful for the most part since tribal community life is so important to many Indians. The whole idea behind the old government policy was to make the American Indians conform to the life-styles of other Americans.

Then came the Wheeler-Howard or Indian Reorganization Act. Its aim was to allow Indian tribes to organize as federally chartered corporations capable of engaging in economic enterprise. Seventy-five percent of all Indian tribes chose to come under the act. The right of Indians to govern themselves to some degree was granted. They now had some say in their own destiny, although the final decisions remained with the secretary of the interior. An Indian Arts and Crafts Board was established to preserve and develop Indian culture. Numerous programs were introduced to conserve Indian lands, grant credit to Indian projects, and improve the health of the people on the reservations.

All this resulted in better educational and health facilities and a restored respect for Indian culture and religion. At long last, the U.S. government had conceded that the Indians had a society with worthwhile values and deserved the chance to live as they believed best for themselves. The Indian Reorganization Act was far from perfect, but it was a much-needed New Deal for American Indians.

The depression also had a harsh effect on working

women, who were often new to the work force. They suffered from the old rule of "last hired, first fired." President Roosevelt appointed former social worker Frances Perkins to the post of U.S. secretary of labor. She was the first American female cabinet officer in history, and she worked for the welfare of both male and female workers.

9

DRUMS OF DISCONTENT—
THE SECOND NEW DEAL

Despite the burst of reforms initiated within the first "hundred days," the year 1934 began with the national spirit flagging. Industrial production was declining, and about 20 percent of the labor force was still out of work. The New Deal coalition of businessmen, workers, and farmers seemed to be falling apart. The business and industrial community chafed under the NRA codes and began to turn so strongly against Roosevelt that he would never regain their confidence. Normally conservative people, always suspicious of Roosevelt's intentions, now raised their voices more stridently against him. Herbert Hoover's speeches suggested that the government was growing too powerful and becoming a threat to liberties guaranteed under the Constitution.

In August 1934, the American Liberty League was formed. Conservative lawyers and even Democratic politicians like Al Smith joined with big business to blast the New Deal. They condemned the growing bureaucracy as well as the "Presidential tyranny" of the New Deal. Roosevelt, they said with growing anger, was taking America too far left. But an even more worrisome thunder of discontent was rising from other more radical quarters.

Governor Huey Long of Louisiana, though he supported Roosevelt in 1932, joined the chorus of voices in 1934 complaining that the president wasn't doing enough. He poked savage fun at the president, calling him Prince Franklin, knight of *Nourmahal* (Roosevelt's yacht). Governor Long ridiculed the farm policies of "Lord Corn Wallace (Henry Wallace)" and claimed his own ideas were better than Roosevelt's. Long's own nickname was "Kingfish" because of his slogan "Every man a king." He favored free homesteads, free education, and cheap food. Long felt that every American should be guaranteed an annual income of $2,000 as part of a "Share the Wealth" program. He wanted one-third of the nation's money to be divided up among all the people. It was an old populist theory that economists took a dim view of, but Long was a hero to the poor people. (If Long had lived to 1936, he would have proved a challenge to Roosevelt, but he was assassinated in 1935 by an old enemy.)

Offering another voice of discontent was Upton Sinclair, the muckraking novelist who gained fame in 1906 with a book titled *The Jungle*. The book described the filthy conditions under which men had to work in the slaughterhouses of Chicago. Sinclair tried to stir up sympathy for the downtrodden workers, but most readers felt sorry for the slain animals and worried about the purity of their own food supply. Sinclair's book did much to encourage the enactment of the Meat Inspection Act of 1906 in President Theodore Roosevelt's administration.

In 1934, Sinclair joined the Democratic party and ran for governor on an "End Poverty in California" (EPIC) platform. His ideas were simple. The government should own all the factories, and people should live on big cooperative farms where all contributed to the common good. He urged that the rich be taxed much more than Roosevelt was taxing them and that everybody over sixty be given a pension of $50 a month. Raymond Moley, a New Deal Brain Truster, called the plan "a blessed retreat, back to nature." With his spectacles worn clipped to his nose and his white hair, Sinclair looked like a kindly professor. He wrote *I, Governor of California and How I Ended Poverty*, and 1 million people bought it.

Another elderly voice of discontent belonged to Dr. Francis E. Townsend, a sixty-six-year-old physician from Long Beach, California. Townsend spoke of looking out his window one day and seeing three old ladies rummaging in a garbage pail for food. He was so horrified that he decided to start his crusade to ease the misery of the elderly poor. The 120-pound, slender, cotton-haired Townsend, from a Nebraska farm, quickly set up Townsend clubs to agitate for his ideas. The movement quickly grew to 12,000 clubs, with 3 million official members and about 7 million unofficial ones, headquartered in California but found all over America.

Townsend proposed a gross income tax of 2 percent. The proceeds would go to everybody over sixty as well as to the blind and disabled and widows with dependent children. The monthly pension would be $200, with the stipulation that all the money had to be spent in a month. Townsend believed that pumping all this money into the economy would stimulate business and put America back on the road to prosperity. Townsend's plan was understandably popular with the huge elderly population of California as well as around the country. Economists dismissed it as farfetched, but to the aged poor it sounded like Christmas in July.

A less gentle drumbeat of criticism was now challenging Roosevelt from Royal Oak, Michigan, near Detroit. The Reverend Charles Edward Coughlin had been preaching his version of a Christian solution to the nation's woes for a long time over his immensely popular radio program on station WJR in Detroit. Coughlin averaged 80,000 fan letters a week, and he needed 150 people just to open his mail. In 1932 he was on Roosevelt's side, but now he turned violently against the president.

A self-taught economist, Coughlin portrayed all bankers as devils and demanded that the government take over everything and employ everybody. He had lost faith in the New Deal, and now he called Roosevelt a "betrayer and a liar" and such choice words as "scab President." Coughlin established his own political party, the National Union for Social Justice. In 1936, it ran North Dakota congressman William Lemke for president.

By the summer of 1933, Adolf Hitler had become the complete master of Germany. He dealt with Germany's devastating depression through nationalizing all its industries, profit sharing, and the abolition of high interest rates. The key to Germany's new prosperity, however, was rooted in rearmament. Industries began to hum with new military contracts. "We will have arms again," declared Hitler.

Visitors to Germany were surprised to see the change as a dispirited people were suddenly revitalized and hopeful. They began to draw comparisons to America's continuing economic misery. Why was everything going so much better in Germany? they asked.

Hitler gained the vocal admiration of more than a few Americans. Lawrence Dennis, a former Wall Street banker from Exeter and Harvard, wrote *The Coming of American Fascism*. Many American college students visited Germany to see vast groups of marching, singing youth on fire with this new revolution. The American Fascist movement gained some converts. Even the virulent anti-Semitism movement in Germany found expression in

America as many radical movements offering solutions to the depression adopted anti-Jewish slogans.

Other Americans turned to communism. The Communist newspaper the *Daily Worker* denounced "that cripple Roosevelt" and hoped that growing disappointment with the New Deal would create opportunities at last for the American Communist revolution. "Comes the day," Communists whispered hopefully to one another.

In September 1934, Roosevelt gave a fireside chat. He tried to appease the business people who thought he'd gone too far. He praised "fair private profit" and tried to calm those voices suggesting he was a socialist, after all, who would abolish private enterprise. To those who felt the New Deal wasn't going far enough, like Long, Townsend, Sinclair, and Coughlin, the president pledged more programs. And even more serious trouble was brewing for the New Deal over at the Supreme Court. A major test of the constitutionality of the NIRA would soon come before the largely conservative Justices.

On May 6, 1935, the Works Progress Administration (WPA) was introduced. Although Harold Ickes was the formal head, Roosevelt wasn't about to make the same mistake twice. He wasn't going to let Ickes look at another bunch of projects through his magnifying glass. The real power of the WPA went to Harry Hopkins. Here was a man after Roosevelt's own heart. Hopkins got the immediate authority to put as many as 5 million jobless men and women to work. "Boys," crowed Hopkins to some colleagues, "this is our hour. We've got to get everything we want, a work program, Social Security, everything! It's now or never."

The average monthly number of people employed by the WPA was two million. The WPA developed 250,000 projects, from large airports to stone walls around universities. Most of the money—about 80 percent—went to public construction, like new post offices and roads. Decades later, Americans can stop to look at the construction date of the corner post office or a small bridge at a crossroads and they would find the telltale date—sometime in the 1930s. These were built with the hands of WPA workers, exposing the oft-told lie that all they really did was rake up leaves or lean on their shovels.

But there were also WPA artistic projects. Hopkins insisted that musicians, artists, writers, and even historians had just as much right as anybody else to a federally sponsored job.

The part of the WPA that gave jobs to writers who had no chance of selling their work to private enterprise was called the Federal Writers' Project. Writers were put to work writing local histories, surveys, and studies. The state histories written during this period form an invaluable resource for all time. Young writers interviewed people who might never have been interviewed, gathering firsthand accounts of the period for generations of historians to learn from.

The Federal Arts Project under the WPA rented theaters for unemployed actors and let them put on plays. Many theaters had gone dark in the depression, so the owners were only too glad to lease their empty buildings to the government. Two-thirds of all the legitimate theaters had gone dark in 1931. The Federal Theatre was not bound by commercial considerations, so the players and producers were freer than they had ever been. They could do poetic dramas like T. S. Eliot's *Murder in the Cathedral* and Marlowe's *Dr. Faustus*. Sinclair Lewis's attack on fascism, *It Can't Happen Here*, the historical play *Abe Lincoln in Illinois*, and even a jazz version of Gilbert and Sullivan's *Mikado* with an all-black cast were staged. Plays were performed in twenty-eight states, allowing many rural audiences to see a live play for the first time in their lives.

But the players stuck their necks out too far when they produced *The Cradle Will Rock*, an attack on corruption in big business. All of a sudden the bureaucrats in Washington got nervous. There had been nasty rumors for some time that the Federal Theatre had become a haven for Communists and other radicals, and now a nervous Washington pulled the plug on *Cradle*.

It was a nice, balmy evening in May in New York as the large audience gathered to see *Cradle*. When they heard of the cancellation, they began to leave, but the actors, Orson Welles and John Houseman, begged them to stay while desperate pleas by phone were made to Washington. When Washington wouldn't budge, Welles called the Jolson Theatre in New York and asked if the play could be shown there. The Jolson Theatre hadn't had a booking in four months, and they were glad for the business. So the actors led their audience in a march onto Broadway, up Seventh Avenue to Fifty-ninth Street. Many others joined the march, and the audience for the play swelled to overflowing the sidewalks. The Jolson Theatre was filled when the curtain went up on a bare stage. The house lights were lowered, and *Cradle* was performed. Though the circumstances were less than ideal, it was described as an exciting, magical evening.

In 1936, 5,000 artists were employed by the government, too. The federal government became the greatest patron of the arts in U.S. history. Conservatives griped at this "waste of tax money," but the arts flourished in every region. Two-thirds of the most important sculptors in America were on the federal rolls.

Social themes prevailed, such as blighted farms in the dust bowl, sharecroppers, and broken-down houses. As concert halls, opera houses, and nightclubs closed during the depression, the WPA orchestras blossomed to save thousands of musicians from despairing idleness. WPA live entertainment came to small towns and brought more shows than the people had seen even in good times; 150,000 concerts were enjoyed by about 100 million people between 1935 and 1940. The federal government even made memorable documentary movies, including *The River*, showing the shameful waste of human and natural resources, and *The Plow That Broke the Land*, a tribute to democratic cooperation among people.

In May 1935, the Rural Electrification Administration was established to stretch power lines into rural areas that never had them before. WPA labor was used to give thousands of people the convenience of electricity.

That month the Wagner, or National Labor Relations, Act was signed. The Wagner Act was much stronger in its support for labor unions than the NIRA. Under the Wagner Act, company unions—groups organized by management that actually worked for the interests of the workers and not the company—were virtually banned. Unfair company practices that had made it hard to form a union were forbidden. For example, some companies fired employees who tried to start or join a union. Then they put their names on so-called *blacklists* so that other companies wouldn't hire them, either.

The Wagner Act was hailed as a bill of rights for labor, for it laid out how unions should be formed and how they might gain recognition by an employer as the sole bargaining agent of his employees. According to the Wagner Act, employees met and chose a union to represent them by secret ballot. When a majority of the employees in an industry, shop, or craft so met and chose their union, that union had the right to bargain with the employer on behalf of all the workers. The Wagner Act put the power of the federal government for the first time strongly on the side of labor.

As if Roosevelt's reputation with the rich was not

shaky enough, he signed the Public Utilities Holding Company Act of 1935, forbidding the creation of huge companies that could control most of a public utility, such as electricity or natural gas. Most agreed with Roosevelt that public utilities were too vital to the public welfare to be under the power of a few rich men, but his Revenue Act of 1936 sent shock waves through the ranks of the upper classes. It was called the wealth tax bill, and it allowed the government to take as much as 70 percent of large incomes. Dubbed the ultimate "soak the rich" program, many said Americans could never again accumulate the huge fortunes they had built in the past.

As an almost direct response to the elderly who supported Sinclair and Townsend, President Roosevelt signed, in the summer of 1935, the law he identified as the supreme achievement of his administration—the Social Security Act. Years before, in a campaign speech in Detroit, he had told this story:

"I shall tell you what sold me on old age insurance," he began. He said he'd returned to his hometown of Hyde Park one winter to discover that tragedy had struck some beloved old friends. They were three brothers and their sister, all in their eighties. "They all shared a farm that was heavily mortgaged. It seems one of the old men fell and died in a snowdrift. The remaining three old folks couldn't cope with this loss plus all the debts. The two old men were taken and put in the county workhouse. The old lady, for want of a better place, was sent to an insane asylum." Then Roosevelt added sadly, "Although she was not insane but just old! That sold me on the idea of trying to keep homes intact for old people."[1]

The Social Security Act provided help for the states in caring for those over sixty-five who came too late to participate in the program. Moreover, a nationwide system of old-age insurance to which both employers and employees contributed was established. Benefits were scheduled to begin in 1942. Also, as part of the program there was unemployment insurance so that people out of work received some income while they searched for a new job. To the end of his life, Roosevelt was proud of the promise he kept to older people by the Social Security Act. Never again would elderly Americans face the stark terror of having no income or of being unable to work, deprived of savings by illness, bad luck, or other circumstances. The act rendered a sense of dignity to them and to many future generations.

As the summer of 1935 passed into history, there were two more programs designed to reform and provide relief. The Banking Act of 1935 gave the Federal Reserve Board the authority to regulate interest rates. This was an important tool for the federal government. When the economy slowed down, interest rates could be lowered, making borrowing easier and stimulating the economy. When the economy heated up and inflation threatened, the government could hike interest rates and cool off the buying spree. The federal government had a new set of controls on the economy. Not everyone applauded this. Was it really capitalism anymore if the government could turn the spigot of money on and off?

Finally, the National Youth Administration (NYA) was created to keep high school and college students out of the labor force: 750,000 students were able to earn $5 to $30 a month by remaining in school and working there as typists, laboratory, and library assistants, and tutors. Most of these programs were directed by Harry Hopkins. He believed that government had to provide for anybody who couldn't find work in private enterprise. A survey in July 1935 in *Fortune* magazine found that 76.8 percent of all Americans agreed.

And so the second New Deal was winding down and President Roosevelt had produced an amazing mass of legislation to provide Americans with relief, reform, and reconstruction.

Still, the depression lingered. The road to recovery still had many obstacles. To Roosevelt, one of the biggest obstacles would be the Supreme Court.

10

A LAST ACT AND ASSESSMENT

The Schechter Poultry case had reached the Supreme Court and was waiting for a verdict. The poultry company complained that it shouldn't be bound by the codes imposed by the NRA because it did business intrastate, in New York, and the federal government had no constitutional right to control trade *within* states—only trade that was interstate or between states. Furthermore, lawyers for the poultry company argued that the NRA gave the executive branch of government too much power.

The Supreme Court included four justices who believed firmly in social Darwinism—that is, that society is best served when government keeps its nose out of people's business. They took a dim view of massive government programs like the NRA. The court also included three so-called liberal judges who were generally favorable to the New Deal. The last three, called centrists, sometimes voted conservative and sometimes liberal.

On May 27, 1935, the Supreme Court voted in favor of the Schechter Poultry Company and struck down the NIRA as unconstitutional. The court's decision was unaminous—all the justices, even the liberal ones, had effectively struck down the blue eagle.

President Roosevelt denounced the decision as "a horse and buggy definition of interstate commerce laws." The president muttered against the "nine old men" of the court who, he feared, might strike down many of his New Deal programs, even Social Security. As 1935 came to a close, hundreds of lawsuits against various New Deal programs (nicknamed Alphabet Soup since they were known mostly by initials like NRA, AAA, etc.) were making their way toward the Supreme Court.

Although the Supreme Court upheld some of the programs, like TVA, Roosevelt was genuinely alarmed. It looked as if the New Deal could be dismantled, piece by piece. Since justices of the Supreme Court tend to live a long time and are not compelled to retire at any age, there seemed no relief in sight. There had been no vacancies on the court during Roosevelt's first three years, and he feared he could now do nothing but sit by and watch his programs shot down like hapless ducks on the first day of hunting season. But Roosevelt was not the sort of man to sit idly by in any crisis, so he began to hatch a plot to make an end run around the "nine old men." But first the president had to win another election.

As the presidential election year of 1936 opened, the Republicans met in Cleveland, Ohio, in June to choose Kansas Governor Alfred (Alf) Landon as their candidate. A clever, folksy man, Landon was in the progressive wing of the Republican party. He had once belonged to Theodore Roosevelt's liberal Bull Moose forces. Landon would not denounce the New Deal because, if elected, he planned to give it a new name and continue its policies. But an angry Herbert Hoover didn't agree. He appeared at the convention to give a fiery speech that brought the party faithful stomping and shouting to their feet. Continued rule by New Dealism, charged Hoover, would lead to "violence and outrage—class hatred preached from the White House—even despotism." Other speakers echoed this cry of alarm. They insisted that America had been imperiled by the New Deal and U.S. liberties were being betrayed. Landon, on the other hand, was so reluctant to criticize the New Deal that some grumbled that he was a "me-too New Dealer." In an interview long after the election, Landon said he believed that by and large the New Deal had saved American society.

Although there was plenty of criticism against Roosevelt in 1936, there was no doubt that he would be renominated when the Democrats met in Philadelphia. Most believed victory was in the air, and the mood at the Democratic convention was triumphant.

During the campaign, Republicans pointed out that almost four years of the New Deal had not solved the depression. Nobody could dispute that. There were still nine million unemployed, although when Roosevelt took office, the number was 12.8 million. Roosevelt responded to the criticism by saying things would be even worse without his measures. He pointed to rising farm income and the millions who were benefiting from his relief programs. Besides, organized labor had achieved great strides, and even though a lot of people felt uneasy about the future and even annoyed at increased government intervention into their private lives, those green relief checks were mighty welcome when they came.

In 1936 two-thirds of American newspapers endorsed Landon. Most newspaper publishers came from elite establishment families that enjoyed decades of wealth, so they were unlikely to sympathize with the New Deal's undermining of the richer classes. Groups of businessmen formed to back Landon behind the slogan "Save the American way of life." The Conservative Liberty League campaigned hard against Roosevelt, charging that he was a subversive of American democracy. The *Literary Digest* took a poll that predicted Landon would win by a comfortable margin.

The campaigns were energetic and generally free of heavy mudslinging. Landon made good, forceful speeches, and Roosevelt was at his best—charming, warm, and persuasive.

Despite the *Literary Digest* poll, Landon suspected right along that he didn't have much of a shot at the presidency. (The *Literary Digest* had polled people on the phone, and many voters were too poor to have a telephone.) True, Landon had support from big business, some conservatives, and the newspapers, but Roosevelt seemed to have everybody else. On his way to New York for an appearance, Landon asked the governor of New Jersey what his chances were in that state. "No chance," said the governor. Then Landon asked about his chances in the country. "None," said the governor.

The 1928 Democratic nominee for president, Al Smith, backed Landon. Smith called money under the New Deal "the baloney dollar." But when election day came, few were surprised by the results. Roosevelt had won by a landslide, with Landon carrying just two states, Vermont and Maine, with a total of eight electoral votes. William Lemke of the Union party got 900,000 votes. Socialist Norman Thomas and Communist Earl Browder trailed far behind. Landon had been beaten even more badly than Hoover. Roosevelt got 28 million votes to Landon's 17 million.

The landslide election of 1936 established two long-term trends in American politics. Labor unions and African-Americans had gone solidly for the Democratic ticket. This would remain a major factor for a long time to come.

Franklin Roosevelt had his big vote of confidence, and his party had increased its percentages in both houses of Congress. The popular president could be forgiven for believing he could do just about anything now. And was there a better time to cut those fellows in the Supreme Court down to size? As FDR saw it, they were putting boulders in the path of progress, and he was about to mount a steam shovel to get them out of the way.

After his 1936 victory, the president admitted there was still much wrong in America. "Here is one-third of a nation ill nourished, ill clad and ill housed now," he said. "If we would keep faith with those who had faith in us, if we would make democracy succeed, I say we must act now!" He then hinted that his wonderful plans for a better America would not be halted by the "limitations" of the Constitution.

On February 5, 1937, Roosevelt fired the opening gun of what would be a major battle to change the court. He proposed to bring the Supreme Court—the only one of the three divisions of government not under popular control—under political pressure. The president called it judicial reorganization, and it boiled down to this: For every Supreme Court justice over seventy who didn't retire, Roosevelt would name an additional member to the court. The suggested maximum for the Supreme Court was to be fifteen, not nine. Roosevelt figured that with his six new liberal justices voting alongside the three liberals already there, he'd have a big majority on the court and his programs would be home free. The president called it infusing the court with new blood. He said that the old men on the court had been fitted with glasses of another generation, and they suffered now from blurred vision. They were blind to the needs of the people in the thirties.

But while Roosevelt talked about "new blood," others gave his plan different names. They called it "Court packing" and they accused the president of trying to smash the Constitution.

The Founding Fathers saw the Supreme Court as a stable defender of the U.S. Constitution. Once appointed, the justices could interpret the Constitution without fear of being avenged at the ballot box. Chosen by the president and approved by the Senate, they were free of political pressure. Tampering with the judicial branch of government created a firestorm of protest. A buzzing, stinging hornet's nest of opposition arose almost overnight.

Progressive Democrat Burton Wheeler of Montana denounced Roosevelt as a "would-be dictator." Wheeler recalled the hysteria of World War I when innocent people might have been hung as traitors except for the intervention of the courts. Only the courts stood firm as president and Congress were carried along on a tide of madness during World War I. Now, Wheeler cried, those very courts were under presidential assault. Even the Gallup poll showed that nearly 60 percent of the people opposed changing the size of the Supreme Court.

Those Americans who always mistrusted Roosevelt now had their worst fears confirmed. They felt he was trying to overturn the American system of government. But what really was going through President Roosevelt's mind? Had he allowed the great electoral victory of 1936 to cloud his judgment, and did he truly intend to "pack" the Supreme Court with his supporters? Or was he only trying to send a message to the Supreme Court that they ought to get in step with the more liberal mood of the nation? Whatever it was, a strange thing happened. The court began to take a kinder view of New Deal programs. Fewer were being declared unconstitutional.

Roosevelt's Judiciary Reform Bill was described by the Senate Judiciary Committee as "needless, futile, and utterly dangerous," and it recommended defeat. But the issue quickly died as Franklin Roosevelt got his chance to make his first appointment. By 1941, Roosevelt had named five of his appointees to the nine-man bench. He chose a strong New Dealer, Senator Hugo Black of Alabama, who was approved by the Senate 63 to 16 even though a minor scandal over his previous KKK (Ku Klux Klan) membership arose. In addition to Justices Stanley Reed, William O. Douglas, and Frank Murphy, Roosevelt appointed New Dealers Felix Frankfurter and Robert H. Jackson. The Supreme Court had survived intact after the small firestorm of controversy, and FDR, the master politician, had gotten what he wanted, too.

Now a more serious problem arose. In late 1936 the American economy seemed on the upswing. Employment was rising, manufacturing was up, and more orders were coming in. But in September 1937, another slump came. Credit restrictions and reduced federal spending were blamed. The economy threatened to plunge steeply once more. Panic struck Roosevelt as the prices on the farm skidded, and some were calling this new crisis the "Roosevelt Recession."

In February 1938 a new Agricultural Adjustment Act (the Supreme Court had struck down the old one) was passed, and farmers could make new loans and receive soil-conservation payments. A floor was established below which farm prices couldn't fall. The Surplus Marketing Administration hurriedly brought up the food surpluses and distributed them to families on relief and school lunch programs. The Food Stamp Plan allowed relief families to get fifty cents' worth of free food for every dollar spent in any grocery store. A family of four in Cleveland filled two half bushel baskets a week with such surplus food as apples, potatoes, bacon, and nuts.

Still, the recession deepened toward another depression. Roosevelt's critics turned on him with new fury. Even old supporters like the NRA's General Johnson joined in the chorus of criticism. Undaunted, Roosevelt authorized new slum-relief projects, tearing down old, defective buildings and erecting new apartments. Memphis saw its "greasy plank" district replaced by a new housing project. The same happened at "Whisky Island" in Cleveland and Atlanta's "Beaver Slide." Fourteen hundred families moved into new units in the Bronx.

The Fair Labor Standards Act of June 1938 was the last major reform law of the New Deal. It provided for a gradually imposed minimum wage of 40¢ an hour and a maximum work week of forty hours. Time-and-a-half had to be paid for overtime. Child labor was banned, and workers under eighteen had to be excluded from dangerous jobs.

The president had done his best now to Prime the Pumps (New Deal economist John Maynard Keynes's idea that in time of economic trouble, government must pour in federal money just as a farmer trying to draw up well water must add water at the top). Now Roosevelt turned to reorganization of the executive branch of government. He added assistants and created two new departments, Public Works and Social Welfare. The *Chicago Tribune* called it the "dictator" plan and said Roosevelt was up to his old tricks of trying to become the tyrant of Pennsylvania Avenue. The bill went down to defeat in a tornado of opposition.

Roosevelt then turned his wrath against those he felt were monopolizing industries and controlling copper and steel to the detriment of the nation. He thundered, "A few powerful men overshadow our economic life," and he swore to control these "blindly selfish men."

Public hearings were conducted in 1938 to see if the monopolies were as bad as the president suggested. The hearings revealed that 200 corporations did control one-half of the nation's industrial wealth and one-fifth of its total wealth. Extremely wealthy corporations held 93 percent of the transportation system, 78 percent of financial institutions, and 66 percent of manufacturing. One aluminum corporation controlled the whole aluminum industry. Three auto firms (General Motors, Ford, and Chrysler) made 86 percent of all cars. All this had come about through mergers of small companies into ever larger single corporations.

This was proof to the president and others that big business had grown into a dangerous monster. But not everybody agreed with that conclusion. Many argued that big was necessary and that the American economy had been healthy, creative, and efficient before the depression. Big corporations had brought about reasonable prices for most products, so why dismantle them? Roosevelt didn't get far with his trust-busting measures, not even in his own party. In fact, disloyal Democrats who effectively opposed him infuriated Roosevelt. He began speaking of getting such people out of the party. He was promptly accused of "purge" tactics (a reference to how the Communist party in Russia purged, or got rid of, disloyal party members). Conservative Democrats called Roosevelt the "new Napoleon" and a "power-drunk dictator."

By the early months of 1939, the economic reforms of the New Deal were put on the back burner as America faced a new challenge. Adolf Hitler had rearmed Germany, and now he had begun his aggressive march across Europe. Czechoslovakia was divided up, and it was only a matter of time before German armies swept through Europe. Japan had invaded Manchuria, and Italy conquered Ethiopia. These three nations, Germany, Japan, and Italy, would form a bloc, called the Axis powers, against the rest of the world. As another world conflagration threatened, Roosevelt turned his attention to foreign policy. Gradually, as America, too, began to manufacture materials for the war ahead, the depression finally ended. Full employment would arrive with the 1940s as Americans rushed to provide the tanks and planes to fight World War II.

•   •   •

The New Deal lasted from March 1933 to the end of 1938. Even today there is a wide assortment of opinions as to how well President Roosevelt dealt with the Great Depression. Critics are quick to point out that in 1939 there were still 8,700,000 Americans out of work. They also argue that the New Deal created an expensive and complicated bureaucracy that would haunt the nation for generations to come. The New Deal doubled the national debt in less than ten years.

Defenders of the New Deal point to what a catastrophic economy did to Russia, Germany, and Italy. It led to brutal tyrannies and the loss of human rights. The New Deal had helped the American people through terrible times while leaving intact the precious American birthright of freedom. The New Deal may not have ended the depression, its defenders admit, but it saved American democracy. What's more, the unemployed were not allowed to sink into hopelessness. They were given wages and worthwhile work to do. Such programs as the CCC and the NYA gave the young a new lease on life and saved farmers from ruin. Furthermore, humane programs like Social Security and unemployment insurance were put into effect so that the elderly and unemployed would never again face total destitution in hard times.

The lasting impact of the New Deal may be found in Social Security and unemployment insurance, minimum wages and maximum hours, housing for low-income people, and federally guaranteed savings accounts. These now permanent programs add immeasurably to the quality of life and peace of mind of just about every American.

Could another program have worked better, faster? We will probably never know. But without a doubt the New Deal forever changed the way Americans look at their government. More importantly, a dramatic breakthrough was made in how the federal government for the first time assumed responsibility for the economic well-being of the nation. In past times of social and economic upheaval, people looked to local or private agencies for help. Ever since the time of Franklin Roosevelt, people have looked to the federal government to guide, direct, and assist the national economy.

Franklin Roosevelt once said, "If we do not have the courage to lead the American people where they want to go, someone else will." The American people of the 1930s made it eminently clear that they wanted to follow where the New Deal led. And this is how most survived the Great Depression—and how American democracy itself triumphed.

HIGHLIGHTS OF
THE GREAT DEPRESSION
AND THE NEW DEAL

PHOTOGRAPHY CREDITS

NOTES

BIBLIOGRAPHY

INDEX

HIGHLIGHTS OF
THE GREAT DEPRESSION
AND THE NEW DEAL

1929
October 24—The U.S. stock market crashes.

1930
June 17—The United States Congress passes the Smoot-Hawley Tariff Bill, the highest protective tariff act in the nation's history.

1932
May through July—The Bonus Expeditionary Force, made up of thousands of World War I veterans, arrives in Washington to demand early payment of their bonus checks; their demonstrations are repulsed by government troops.
November 8—Franklin Delano Roosevelt is elected to his first term as president.

1933
January 30—Adolf Hitler becomes chancellor of Germany, beginning a twelve-year rule as dictator of the Third Reich.
March 4—Roosevelt is inaugurated the thirty-second president of the United States.
March 6—Congress passes the Emergency Banking Act, which empowered the government to stabilize and reform the American banking system.
March 31—President Roosevelt creates the Civilian Conservation Corps under the Unemployment Relief Act. The Corps hired 250,000 unemployed young men to work for the government.

April 19—President Roosevelt lifts the gold standard.

May 12—The president creates the Federal Emergency Relief Act, which enabled the government to provide direct relief to states, cities, towns, and counties. He also creates the Agricultural Adjustment Act, which gave relief to farmers and revamped farm economic policies, and the Emergency Farm Mortgage Act, which refinanced farms threatened by foreclosure.

May 18—The Tennessee Valley Authority Act creates a system of dams and reservoirs to assist economic development and reclamation in the Tennessee River valley.

May 27—The Truth-in-Securities Act is created to reform abuses in the buying and selling of stocks and bonds.

June 13—The Home Owners Loan Act is created to refinance residential homes threatened by foreclosure.

June 16—Congress passes the U.S. National Industrial Recovery Act, which empowered the National Recovery Administration to draft industrial codes designed to achieve recovery and reform.

1935

May 6—The president creates the Works Progress Administration, which undertook extensive building projects and provided work to the unemployed.

May 27—The U.S. Supreme Court declares the National Industrial Recovery Act of 1933 unconstitutional in its ruling on the Schechter Poultry Corporation case.

May—The president establishes the Rural Electrification Administration to advance the spread of electricity to rural areas. The president also signs the Public Utility Holding Act, which assured fair availability of public utilities to all.

July 5—The National Labor Relations Act, also called the Wagner Act, affirms the right of laborers to organize and bargain collectively.

August 14—The president signs into law the Social Security Act, which provided a nationwide system of insurance and benefits for Americans over the age of sixty-five and for the unemployed.

August—The Banking Act of 1935 is created for the purpose of reorganizing the Federal Reserve System.

1936

November 8—Franklin Roosevelt is elected to a second term.

1938

June—Congress passes the last major reform law of the New Deal. The Fair Labor Standards Act provided a minimum hourly wage and a ceiling over work hours for laborers.

PHOTOGRAPHY CREDITS

Photographs courtesy of: UPI/Bettmann Newsphotos: pp. 1 top, 3 top, 5 center, 8 top, 13; AP/Wide World Photos: pp. 1 bottom, 2, 3 bottom, 5 top and bottom, 7 bottom, 8 bottom, 9 top, 10 top, 11 bottom, 12, 14; Magnum Photos: p. 4; The Bettmann Archive: p. 6; Culver Pictures: 7 top, 9 bottom, 15; U.S.D.A.: p. 10 bottom; Historical Picture Service: 11 top; Archives of Labor and Urban Affairs, Wayne State University: p. 16.

NOTES

Chapter One
Storm Clouds Gather

The material on the twenties is taken from W. E. Leuchtenburg, *The Perils of Prosperity*—1914–1932 (Chicago: University of Chicago, 1958); Richard Hofstadter, *The United States: The History of a Republic* (New Jersey: Prentice-Hall, 1960), 628, 644; T. Saloutos and J. D. Hicks, *Twentieth Century Populism: Agricultural Discontent in the Middle West 1900–1939* (Madison: University of Wisconsin Press, 1951); Samuel Eliot Morison, *The Oxford History of the American People* (New York: Oxford University Press, 1965), 888, 934. Editors of *Time* magazine and George J. Church, "The Wealth of Nations," *The Most Amazing 60 Years in History, Time Anniversary Issue*. 60th Anniversary Issue, 101, 105; John Maynard Keynes, *The Economic Consequences of the Peace* (New York: Harcourt Brace & World, 1920); Charles A. Lindbergh, *The Spirit of St. Louis* (New York: Scribners, 1956).

Chapter Two
The Bubble Bursts

1. "Bankers v. Panic," *Time 60th Anniversary Issue*, 5 October 1983, 104.
2. "Crash Maroons Tourists," *Los Angeles Times*, 30 October 1929.
3. Material on impact on businessmen from: Studs Terkel, *Hard Times* (New York: Pantheon, 1970), 79, 103.
4. Material on depression in Germany and Hitler from Alan Bullock, *Hitler, A Study in Tyranny* (New York: Bantam, 1961).

General material on the Crash taken from John K. Galbraith, *The Great Crash* (Boston: Houghton Mifflin, 1959). Material on President Hoover from Herbert Hoover, *Memoirs: The Great Depression, 1929–1941*, Vol. 3 (New York: Macmillan, 1952); Dorothy McGee, *Herbert Hoover: Engineer, Humanitarian, Statesman* (New York: Dodd, 1965); William S. Myers and W. H. Newton, *The Hoover Administration* (New York: Scribners, 1936); Harris G. Warren, *Herbert Hoover and the Great Depression* (New York: Oxford University Press, 1959); Babson incident described on p. 939 of Samuel Eliot Morison, *The Oxford History of the American People* (New York: Oxford University Press, 1965).

Chapter Three
The Depression Deepens

1. Richard C. Wade, *Negroes in American Life* (Boston: Houghton Mifflin, 1965), 157–74.
2. Studs Terkel, *Hard Times* (New York: Pantheon, 1970), 462–68.
3. Studs Terkel, *Hard Times*, 261–65.
4. Marquis James, *Biography of a Bank* (New York: Harper, 1954), 355.

Chapter Four
The Rise and Fall of the Bonus Army

Material on the Bonus Army is taken from Willard A. Heaps, *Riots USA: 1765–1970* (New York: Seabury Press, 1970), 131, 137; William S. Myers and W. H. Newton, *The Hoover Administration* (New York: Scribners, 1936), 64–69, 119–20, 267–68, 498, 501; "The Saddest March," *American Heritage*, Vol. 14, June 1963; Studs Terkel, *Hard Times* (New York: Pantheon, 1970), 27–32, 325–30.

Chapter Five
The March to Victory

1. Giannini incident from p. 361 of Marquis James book.
2. Fish information from pp. 331–37 Studs Terkel book.
3. Frances Perkins quote from Edwin C. Rozwenc, *The New Deal, Revolution or Evolution* (Boston: D. C. Heath, 1959), foreword, and Frances Perkins, *The Roosevelt I Knew* (New York: Viking, 1946), 330.
4. Jane Polley, ed., *American Folklore and Legend* (Pleasantville, N.Y.: Reader's Digest Association, 1978), 387.

Material on Franklin Roosevelt from Catherine Owens, *The FDR Story* (New York: Crowell, 1962); Frank Freidel, *Franklin D. Roosevelt*, 3 vols. (Boston: Little, Brown, 1952–56); on Al Smith: Oscar Handlin, *Al Smith and His America* (Boston: Little, Brown, 1958). Material on 1932 campaign taken from Denis M. Brogan, *The Era of Franklin Roosevelt* (New Haven: Yale University Press, 1950). Herbert Hoover, *The Challenge to Liberty* (New York: Scribners, 1934). Material on Eleanor Roosevelt from Eleanor Roosevelt, *This I Remember* (New York: Harper, 1949). Eleanor Roosevelt, *The Autobiography of Eleanor Roosevelt* (New York: Harper, 1961).

Chapter Six
The First "Hundred Days"—Part One

Material on the early New Deal taken from Edwin Rozwenc, *The New Deal: Revolution or Evolution* (Boston: D. C. Heath, 1959); Arthur M. Schlesinger, Jr., *The Age of Roosevelt: The Politics of Upheaval* (Boston: Houghton Mifflin, 1960); Dixon Wecter, *The Age of the Great Depression* (New York: Macmillan, 1948). Material on Wall Street corruption: F. T. Pecora, *Wall Street Under Oath* (New York: Simon and Schuster, 1939). Material on Judge Bradley incident, pp. 255–61 *Hard Times*.

Chapter Seven
The First "Hundred Days"—Part Two

1. *Hard Times*, p. 279.
2. John Steinbeck, *The Grapes of Wrath* (New York: Viking, 1939): Material on AAA and farm problems from *Agricultural Discontent in the Middle West*; S. I. Rosenman, ed., *The Public Papers and Addresses of Franklin D. Roosevelt* (New York: Random House and Harper, 1938–50). *The Age of the Great Depression; Hard Times.*

Material on the TVA from D. E. Lilienthal, *TVA* (New York: Harper, 1944); R. L. Neuberger and S. B. Kahn, *Integrity: George W. Norris* (New York: Vanguard, 1937). Material on Hopkins from Robert E. Sherwood, *Roosevelt and Hopkins* (New York: Harper, 1948). Material on Ickes from Harold Ickes, *Back to Work: PWA* (New York: Macmillan, 1935). Material on the NRA from Hugh S. Johnson, *The Blue Eagle: From Egg to Earth* (New York: Doubleday, 1935).

Chapter Eight
Minorities in the Depression

Overview of minorities in the depression taken from Kathleen Wright, *The Other Americans* (Greenwich, Conn.: Fawcett, 1971), 184–207. Material on Indians: Alvin M. Josephy Jr., *The Indian Heritage of America* (New York: Bantam, 1969), 352–55. African-American material: *Negroes in American Life*, 157, 179, and *Hard Times*, pp. 498, 502. On Mexican-Americans, *Hard Times*.

Chapter Nine
Drums of Discontent—The Second New Deal

1. Rozwenc, *The New Deal*, pp. 46–48.
Material on the individuals forming anti-Roosevelt movements from Andrew Rolle, *California* (New York: Crowell, 1963), 510–18; Charles J. Tull, *Father Coughlin and the New Deal* (Syracuse: Syracuse University Press, 1965); James M. Burns, *Roosevelt: The Lion and the Fox* (New York: Harcourt, 1956). Material on the WPA artists projects from *Hard Times*, 417–38. General material about laws from Raymond Moley, *After Seven Years* (New York: Harper, 1939). Schlesinger books.

Chapter Ten
A Last Act and Assessment

Material primarily from Carl B. Swisher, *American Constitutional Development* (Boston: Houghton Mifflin, 1943); Herman Pritchett, *The Roosevelt Court—1937–1947* (New York: Macmillan, 1948).

BIBLIOGRAPHY

Books

Allen, Frederick. *Since Yesterday: The Nineteen-Thirties in America.* New York: Harper, 1940.

Brogan, Denis M. *The Era of Franklin Roosevelt.* New Haven: Yale University Press, 1950.

Brown, Josephine C. *Public Relief: 1929–39.* New York: Holt, 1940.

Bullock, Alan. *Hitler, A Study in Tyranny.* New York: Bantam, 1961.

Burns, James M. *Roosevelt: The Lion and the Fox.* New York: Harcourt, 1956.

Eccles, Marriner S. *Beckoning Frontiers.* New York: Knopf, 1951.

Freidel, Frank. *Franklin D. Roosevelt.* 3 vols. Boston: Little, Brown, 1952–56.

Galbraith, John K. *The Great Crash.* Boston: Houghton Mifflin, 1959.

Handlin, Oscar. *Al Smith and His America.* Boston: Little, Brown, 1958.

Heaps, Willard A. *Riots, USA: 1765–1970.* New York: Seabury Press, 1970.

Hofstadter, Richard. *The United States: The History of a Republic.* New Jersey: Prentice Hall, 1960.

Hoover, Herbert. *Memoirs: The Great Depression, 1929–1941.* Vol. 3. New York: Macmillan, 1952.

_____. *The Challenge to Liberty*. New York: Scribner's, 1934.

Ickes, Harold. *Back to Work: PWA*. New York: Macmillan, 1935.

James, Marquis. *Biography of a Bank*. New York: Harper, 1954.

Johnson, Hugh S. *The Blue Eagle: From Egg to Earth*. New York: Doubleday, 1935.

Keynes, John Maynard. *The Economic Consequences of the Peace*. New York: Harcourt, 1920.

Leuchtenburg, W. E. *The Perils of Prosperity—1914–1932*. Chicago: University of Chicago Press, 1958.

Lilienthal, D. E. *TVA*. New York: Harper, 1944.

Lindbergh, Charles A. *The Spirit of St. Louis*. New York: Scribners, 1956.

McGee, Dorothy. *Herbert Hoover: Engineer, Humanitarian, Statesman*. New York: Dodd, 1965.

Moley, Raymond. *After Seven Years*. New York: Harper, 1939.

Morison, Samuel Eliot. *The Oxford History of the American People*. New York: Oxford University Press, 1965.

Myers, William S., and W. H. Newton. *The Hoover Administration*. New York: Scribners, 1936.

Neuberger, R. L., and S. B. Kahn. *Integrity: George W. Norris*. New York: Vanguard, 1937.

Peare, Catherine Owens. *The FDR Story*. New York: Crowell, 1962.

Pecora, F. T. *Wall Street Under Oath*. New York: Simon & Schuster, 1939.

Perkins, Frances. *The Roosevelt I Knew*. New York: Viking, 1946.

Pritchett, Herman. *The Roosevelt Court—1937–1947*. New York: Macmillan, 1948.

Rolle, Andrew. *California*. New York: Crowell, 1963.

Roosevelt, Eleanor. *This I Remember*. New York: Harper, 1949.

_____. *The Autobiography of Eleanor Roosevelt*. New York: Harper, 1961.

Rosenman, S. I., ed. *The Public Papers and Addresses of Franklin D. Roosevelt*. 13 vols. New York: Random House and Harper, 1938–50.

Rozwenc, Edwin C. *The New Deal: Revolution or Evolution*. Boston: D. C. Heath, 1959.

Saloutos, T., and J. D. Hicks. *Agricultural Discontent in the Middle West 1900–1939.* Madison: University of Wisconsin, 1951.

Schlesinger, Arthur M., Jr. *The Age of Roosevelt: The Crisis of the Old Order—1919–1933.* Boston: Houghton Mifflin, 1957.

————. *The Age of Roosevelt: The Politics of Upheaval.* Boston: Houghton Mifflin, 1960.

Sherwood, Robert E. *Roosevelt and Hopkins.* New York: Harper, 1948.

Swisher, Carl B. *American Constitutional Development.* Boston: Houghton Mifflin, 1943.

Terkel, Studs. *Hard Times.* New York: Pantheon, 1970.

Tull, Charles J. *Father Coughlin and the New Deal.* Syracuse: Syracuse University Press, 1965.

Warren, Harris G. *Herbert Hoover and the Great Depression.* New York: Oxford University Press, 1959.

Wade, Richard C. *Negroes in American Life.* Boston: Houghton Mifflin, 1965.

————. *Cities in American Life.* Boston: Houghton Mifflin, 1971.

Wright, Kathleen. *The Other Americans.* Greenwich, Conn.: Fawcett, 1971.

Magazine Articles

"Bankers v. Panic," from *Time* magazine 60th Anniversary issue. October 1983.
"The Wealth of Nations," from *Time* magazine, 60th Anniversary issue. October 1983.
"Saddest March," from *American Heritage*, Vol. 14, June 1963.

Newspapers

"Crash Maroons Tourists." *Los Angeles Times*, 30 October 1929.
"Stocks Dive Amid Frenzy." *Los Angeles Times*, 30 October 1929.
"Last Bonus Band Ousted: Hoover Praises Troops," *Los Angeles Times*, 30 July 1932.

Palmer, Kyle D. "Banks to Open Today by Order of Roosevelt," *Los Angeles Times*, 11 March 1933.

Francis, Warren B. "President Asks Fifteen-Judge Supreme Court in Shake-up," *Los Angeles Times*, 6 February 1937.

"Sudetenland Given to Hitler," *Los Angeles Times*, 30 September 1938.

INDEX

Abe Lincoln in Illinois, 78
Agricultural Adjustment Act (1933), 58–61
Agricultural Adjustment Act (1938), 90
Agricultural Marketing Act (1929), 25
American Indians, 70–71
American Liberty League, 73
Axis powers, 92–93

Babson, Roger W., 17
Bank holiday (1933), 52
Banking Act (1935), 82
Banking industry, 30–31, 33, 44–45, 47, 52–55, 82
Bankruptcy, 30–31, 33
Bethune, Mary McLeod, 68–69
Black, Hugo, 90
Black Americans, 31–32, 68–69, 87
Bonus Army, 34–40
Bread lines, 23–24, 26, 29, 70
Browder, Earl, 87

Chicago Tribune, 91

Chinese-Americans, 70
Chrysler, Walter P., 13
Churchill, Winston, 66
Civilian Conservation Corps, 55–56, 62
Clayton, Horace, 69
Collective bargaining, 63–64
Collier, John, 70–71
Coming of American Fascism, The, 76
Comingore, Dorothy, 60
Communism, 31, 37–38, 69, 77, 87
Conservative Liberty League, 87
Coolidge, Calvin, 15
Coughlin, Charles E., 45, 75–76
Cradle Will Rock, The, 79

Daily Worker, 77
Dennis, Lawrence, 76
Dr. Faustus, 78
Douglas, William O., 90

Economy Act (1933), 55
Eliot, T. S., 78
Emergency Banking Act (1933), 52

Emergency Farm Mortgage Act (1933), 57
Evictions, 29–30

Fair Labor Standards Act (1938), 91
Farley, James, 43, 67
Farming, 14, 25, 31–32, 44, 57, 58–61, 69, 90
Fascism, 70, 76–77
Federal Arts Project, 78–80
Federal Deposit Insurance Corporation (FDIC), 54
Federal Emergency Relief Act (1933), 57
Federal Emergency Relief Association (FERA), 67
Federal Farm Board, 25
Federal Reserve Board, 82
Federal Surplus Relief Corporation, 60
Federal Trade Commission (FTC), 55
Federal Writers Project, 78
Fish, Hamilton, 46
Foreclosures, 47–48, 57
Fortune, 82
Foster, William Z., 45, 47
Frankfurter, Felix, 90

Garner, John Nance, 42, 43
General Motors, 19
Germany, 24, 30, 31, 70, 92–93
Giannini, A. P., 45
Glass-Steagall Banking Act (1933), 54
Gold standard, 56–57
Grapes of Wrath, The, 60

Harding, Warren, 15
Hitler, Adolf, 24, 31, 76, 92
Hoboes, 20–21
Holiday associations, 32

Home Owner's Loan Corporation (HOLC), 62–63
Hoover, Herbert, 13–14, 15, 16, 21–22, 23, 25, 28, 30, 33, 36–37, 40, 41, 42, 44, 46, 48, 73, 85–86
Hopkins, Harry, 66–67, 77, 78, 82
Houseman, John, 79
Hurley, Patrick J., 39

Ickes, Harold, 66, 77
Indian Reorganization Act, (1933), 71
Industry, 14, 21, 30–31, 63–66, 73, 80, 91–92. See also Banking industry
It Can't Happen Here, 78

Jackson, Robert H., 90
Jewish-Americans, 70
Johnson, Hugh, 63, 65–66, 91
Judiciary Reform Bill, 89–90
Jungle, The, 74

Keynes, John Maynard, 91

La Guardia, Fiorello, 49
Landon, Alfred, 85–87
Lemke, William, 76, 87
Lewis, Sinclair, 78
Lincoln, Abraham, 68
Lindbergh, Charles A., 11
Literary Digest, 87
Long, Huey, 45, 74

MacArthur, Douglas, 39
Meat Inspection Act (1906), 74
Mellon, Andrew, 22, 37
Mikado, 78
Minimum wage, 64, 91–92, 93
Minorities, 31–32, 68–72, 87
Moley, Raymond, 48, 75

Monopolies, 64, 91–92
Morgan, J. P., 18
Movies, 12, 26, 33, 80
Murder in the Cathedral, 78
Murphy, Frank, 90

National Association of
    Manufacturers, 21
National Industrial Recovery Act
    (1933), 63, 65–66, 77, 84–85
National Labor Relations Act
    (1935), 80
National Recovery Administration
    (NRA), 63–66, 73, 84
National Union for Social Justice,
    76
National Youth Administration
    (NYA), 82
New Deal:
    conception of, 44–45, 49
    legislation, 52–67, 71, 77–
        83, 89–90, 91, 93
    minorities and, 68–72
    critics of, 73–83, 88–90, 93
    Supreme Court and, 77,
        84–85, 88–90
    legacy of, 93–94
Norris, George, 61

Pace, John, 38
Patman, C. Wright, 35, 37
Pecora, Ferdinand, 54
Perkins, Francis, 46, 72
Plays, 78–80
Plow That Broke the Land, The, 80
Presidential election (1932), 41–
    49
Presidential election (1936), 85–
    87
Private charities, 20, 22–23
Prohibition, 12
Public Utilities Holding Company
    Act (1935), 81

Public works, 25
Public Works Administration
    (PWA), 66

Radio, 12, 53, 76
Reconstruction Finance
    Corporation, 31
Reed, Stanley, 90
Revenue Act (1936), 81
River, The, 80
Roaring Twenties, 11–12
Rockefeller, John D. Jr., 19
Rogers, Will, 18, 46
Roosevelt, Eleanor, 42, 50–51,
    58, 68
Roosevelt, Franklin D.:
    background, 42–43
    election (1932), 41–49
    first 100 days, 52–67
    and minorities, 68–72, 87
    critics of, 73–83, 88–90, 93
    election (1936), 85–87
    and Supreme Court, 77,
        84–85, 88–90
    legacy of, 93–94
Roosevelt, James, 48
Roosevelt, Theodore, 42, 74, 85
Rural Electrification
    Administration, 80

Salvation Army, 23
Schechter Poultry Company, 84–
    85
Sinclair, Upton, 74–75, 81
Smith, Alfred E., 42, 43, 73, 87
Smoot-Hawley Tariff Bill (1930),
    26
Social Security Act (1935), 81–
    82, 93
Soup kitchens, 23–24, 26, 29, 70
Spreckles Sugar Refinery, 30
Stalin, Joseph, 45
Steinbeck, John, 60

Stock market, 13, 14–15, 17–19, 44, 55
Supreme Court, 77, 84–85, 88–90
Surplus Marketing Administration, 90

Tariff policies, 15–16, 25–26
Tennessee Valley Authority (TVA), 61–62
Thomas, Norman, 46, 47, 87
Time magazine, 13
Townsend, Francis E., 75, 81
Treaty of Versailles, 15
Truth in Securities Act (1933), 55
Tugwell, Rexford G., 48

Unemployment, 20–21, 23–24, 25, 26–27, 28–29, 33, 44, 45, 68, 86, 93

Union party, 87
U.S. Steel, 18, 19

Von Hindenburg, Paul, 30

Wagner Act (1935), 80
Walker, Jimmy, 21
Wallace, Henry A., 59
Wallace's Farmer, 59
Welles, Orson, 79
Wheeler, Burton, 89
Whitney, Richard, 18
Working women, 71–72
Works Progress Administration (WPA), 77–80
World economy, 15, 24, 30, 56–57
World War I, 15, 21, 34
World War II, 92–93